7 Steps TO GET YOUR CHILD READING

7 Steps TO GET YOUR CHILD READING

Louise Park

Illustrated By Nellé May Pierce

ALLEN&UNWIN

SYDNEY•MELBOURNE•AUCKLAND•LONDON

First published by Allen & Unwin in 2020

Allen & Unwin
83 Alexander Street
Crows Nest NSW 2065
Australia
Phone: (61 2) 8425 0100
Email: info@allenandunwin.com
Web: www.allenandunwin.com

With thanks to Lake Press for permission to reproduce material from *The Tent*,
written by Louise Park and illustrated by Noopur Thakur, and *Guess What: Colours*,
by Jeannette Rowe; to Hinkler Books for permission to reproduce material from *Harriet
Clare Mystery Dare*, written by Louise Park and illustrated by Marlene Monterrubio;
and to co-author Susannah McFarlane and illustrator James Hart for permission to
reproduce material from *D-Bot Squad: Dino Hunter*, published by Allen & Unwin.

A catalogue record for this
book is available from the
NATIONAL
LIBRARY   National Library of Australia
OF AUSTRALIA

ISBN 978 1 76052 467 8

Cover and text design by Sandra Nobes
Cover and text illustrations by Nellé May Pierce
Set in 11.5/18 pt Minion Pro by Midland Typesetters
Printed and bound in Australia by Griffin Press, part of Ovato

10 9 8 7 6 5 4 3 2 1

For Sarah and Tim, who taught me everything I know.
You are my sun, my moon and my stars, and always will be.

For Bella, Amelia, Ellie and Evan, my Gen Alpha treasures.
May your kites forever fly high. You bring me more joy
than I'm sure I deserve.

Some random facts about literacy

Children who frequently read develop stronger reading and writing skills.

About half of the words in the English language can be phonetically sounded out.

Children who start school with no or minimal literacy skills can struggle to close the gap with their peers, and that gap may continue to grow. Furthermore, they may never catch up unless they are identified and supported as early as possible.

A child's oral language and vocabulary are key early predictors of learning-to-read success.

A child needs to hear a word around 250 times before they will remember it.

Over 44% of Australians have literacy levels below what is considered enough to get by in everyday life, according to the Australian Bureau of Statistics. That is, their literacy skills are so poor that they cannot cope with the tasks of everyday life, such as filling in forms and accessing important information.

Contents

I am a fighter,
an adventurer, a dancer.
I am a wizard, a lion,
a leader, a dreamer.

I AM A READER

-GEORGIA, 13
@ @georgia_iamdyslexic

Introduction:

Generation Alpha

- -

It is 2011, and Addie is just seventeen months old. She walks up to my television and tries to swipe the screen with her index finger as though it were a gigantic iPad. I watch her, amazed by what this tiny child is doing, but I also find the moment so adorable that I grab my iPhone so that I can video her. I fumble with the settings as I move the camera to video-mode, and in those few seconds she's turned and seen me with the phone, and she wants it. Oh, how she wants it. I set the phone to flight mode and hand it over.

The excitement is beyond anything any other item I have could elicit. Addie's dimpled fingers dexterously pinch, tap and swipe the screen, and the room fills with her babbles and squeals of delight. But for me, the delight is short-lived. The internal cross-examination has begun, and I'm drowning in carer/babysitter guilt. *Why did you give her the stupid iPhone? You're a children's*

1

author and educator. You know the issues with screen time, you're colluding with the enemy, and you're not even ensuring that it's quality screen time!

Next, the alarmist news reporting scurries across my brain.

Technology is destroying our children's brains!

It's time to admit that screens are just digital pacifiers!

Kids are addicted to screens and parents and carers are to blame!

I'm to blame. I'm a bad carer. I'm rotting this child's brain by giving in, and she's not even mine! But is it true? Is it really so bad for them?

My internal chatter gets the better of me and the alarmists win, this time. So I try to do the right thing. I attempt distraction techniques so that I can extract the iPhone from her grasp. But the battle was lost the moment I handed it over. Of course, she cries. And cries.

And all the while, another part of me is marvelling at the sheer cleverness of this little girl. Her knowledge of technology at such a young age impresses me. There, I've said it. I am seriously impressed. In fact, it blows my mind. And in all of this, it strikes me how different this child's early years are going to be from my own children's in the late 1980s and early '90s, and how even more starkly different they will be from mine.

. . . .

Addie is a Generation Alpha child. Anyone born from 2010 up to 2030 will land in the Gen Alpha cohort, and according to statistics, 2.5 million Alphas are born around the globe every week.

If ever a generation had a hallmark first year of births, it's this one. Think about this: 2010 was the first year that Gen Alphas began being born. It was also the year the iPad was introduced, Instagram was created and 'app' was the new buzzword.

These Alpha kids will be the first generation to grow up with iPads and tablets in their hands. The vast majority will never know what life was like without a smartphone. From a young age they will know how to put their thoughts online in an instant and have them broadcast to the masses, and, unlike any generation before them, they will spend their growing years completely immersed in technology.

Gen Alpha, the only generation to live totally in the twenty-first century, is the swiper, pincher and tapper cohort, and the only generation to interact for the first time with these technologies at extremely young ages. Because they are the first generation to do so, they're like a massive global tech experiment. What does it mean for these children to have screens placed in front of them from the get-go as entertainers, educational toys and, at worst, placators? How does it impact on their literacy acquisition? Their learning? Their socialising? Their lives?

But this book isn't so much about technology as it is about how we can ensure our Generation Alpha children become literate in an environment where reading competes with many more interactive claimers of their time. It's about how we harness all that is important for building competent readers and lifelong learners. It's about the steps that will give them the best shot at success, because Gen A are the group most at risk in the literacy stakes – many of them are already struggling.

The goalposts have shifted for them, their parents and caregivers. Gen A are breaking new ground as a result of technological advances, and their parents are having to navigate these uncharted waters.

This book will guide you through these uncharted waters. It will help you restore the balance between screens and reading and show you in seven straightforward steps how to ensure your child has a positive and success-oriented journey to literacy. You will discover how to make this journey fun and pain-free, and how to incorporate it effortlessly into family life. Because, let's face it, life is full-on for today's families – there is so much more to juggle, often with less support than previous generations had. If you know how we learn to read, if you know the best techniques to use when reading with your child, if you are fully armed with the best tips and activities, then you simply cannot fail.

'There is more treasure in books than in all the pirate's loot on Treasure Island.'

- WALT DISNEY

That reading thing

I'm in one of several huge marquees in the grounds of the school hosting the Whitsunday Voices Youth Literature Festival. The school has invited a group of children's authors and illustrators to present to more than 15,000 children who will be bussed in over three big days. It's day two, and I'm up the front having my mic fitted when the first group of children filing into the tent begin calling and waving to me as they take their seats. I step down from the stage to say hello.

A six-year-old boy leaps from his chair and runs to meet me. In a breathless rush he tells me that he has read every Boy vs Beast book I've ever written. I'm about to reply when he launches into a catalogue of the beasts I co-created with my writing buddy, Susannah McFarlane. The level of detail, the knowledge of the beasts' family trees and the recollection of the battle plays astounds me beyond words. I wrote these books, yet I can barely keep up with him in recalling them all. How has he retained all of this?

Before I know it, I'm surrounded by a group of Zac Power Test Drive and Spy Recruit fans, boys and girls. They're all frantically talking at once: 'My favourite gadget is—', 'How funny was it when Zac was hanging from the sky and—', 'You know what Zac should do about—'. I am completely blown away by this reception, and I think, not for the first time, how lucky I am to have the job that I have.

Little do I know the best is yet to come. I feel a tug on my jacket, and I turn to find a group of girls each holding their entire collection of Harriet Clare books. They are so well-loved, they make my heart flip-flop in my chest. One girl holds out her stack of books and tells me that she's here all day and would I sign them for her at lunchtime? I tell her and her friends that I can't wait to sign their books for them, and that I'd absolutely love to read some of their contributions to Harriet's secret notebooks if that would be okay. In response, the girl quickly shows me her favourite page from *Harriet Clare Mystery Dare*, nodding excitedly. I read her contribution to Harriet's secret diary and tell her she's spot on and that she should write the next one. I ask her what she likes most about Harriet. 'She's my best friend!' she squeals, hugging the books to her chest. 'And I just get her, like, heaps and heaps. It's like she's me!'

And just like that, I am undone.

Later, as I finish up and everyone prepares to leave the tent, one of the teachers comes up and says to me, 'That was better than a rock concert!' This comment cracks me up, and I tell her that I will never, ever get over the incredible power and magic of books, and I mean it. That a book can ignite so much joy in children is truly breathtaking, humbling and addictive all at once!

My eyes scan the enormous grounds dotted with marquees, and I watch the sea of beaming faces spilling out from the other tents. They're eager to get to their next session, and I think, hurrah for teachers who know the importance of inspiring their young readers as they navigate their literacy journey. Hurrah for the organisers and their blood, sweat and tears in pulling an event like this together. And I know they all understand the miracle that is this reading thing – the necessary gift that sets a child up for life.

I have been lucky to have spent my entire working life around children in one way or another, locally and in other countries. In my many evolutions throughout my career, I have taught kids, I've taught their teachers, I've published resources for their schools to use with them, and when that wasn't enough, I began writing for them and visiting them in schools, at festivals and events and in bookstores, as a children's author. In all that time, I have never left the preschool and primary school environment.

Just one glance at my author website will tell you that my life's work has and will continue to be focused on helping children learn to read and become strong, confident, lifelong readers. I know that if a child has mastered this when they leave primary school, doors will open. To me, it is the single most important thing we can teach them. If they can read, all other learning will follow.

And I know from experience that the road to literacy isn't always straightforward or pain-free. In my decades spent watching children working away at this reading thing, I feel I've seen it all, and I don't ever take it for granted when a child cracks the code and begins to independently read books. That moment when it all comes together is pure magic. That transformation of lines and squiggles on a page into stories happens seemingly effortlessly for some, yet it's an almost never-ending struggle for others – with some of these children never learning to read at a level where they can function adequately in life.

For these children, reading feels like a big magic trick that they've not been told the secret to, and so they can't perform it. What's even more distressing is that this group is growing – it's getting bigger when it should be disappearing.

Why is this? And more importantly, how can you ensure your Gen A child doesn't become one of those left stranded?

Is there a secret formula for teaching your child to read?

Let me say from the outset: I do not believe there is one magical technique for learning to read. It isn't a one-size-fits-all scenario. What works with one child may need to be rejigged to accommodate another.

Nor do I believe there is a 'use-by date' for acquiring literacy. Children learn in their own time at their own pace. They learn to walk and talk at different rates, and it's the same with reading and writing.

However, while there may not be one magical formula, there is definitely a set of ingredients for reading success. It takes more than one ingredient to build a strong, competent reader, and these ingredients are like a jigsaw – it is not complete until all the pieces are in place. No one piece should be left out.

The good news is these ingredients are easy and cheap to include in your child's reading journey, and they are all to be found within the pages of this book. Every parent needs to know what these ingredients are, why they need to be used together and how to go about weaving them effortlessly into their child's everyday life. Because parents and carers are, and always will be, a child's greatest and most valuable teacher and resource.

Learning to read is actually darn hard!

So, let's start at the beginning: the act of reading. What is it and what are our brains doing when we read?

Learning to read is truly extraordinary. Children are mastering an extremely complicated process that involves looking at weird black marks on a page and constructing meaning from them. While that might sound simple and straightforward, it's actually no mean feat. But when they have early success with it, they naturally want to read more. Reading more means they'll go on to become confident and engaged readers. And that's what we want.

Competent readers don't think twice about reading. We just do it. Most of us won't even remember how we learnt to do it: we just can. Right now, you are reading my sentences here without any effort at all. And you're quick at it. Your eyes take in all the letter shapes, words and punctuation marks automatically, and, quick as a flash, you know the message they're delivering – you make meaning from it all. It's probably been a very long time since you were aware of using reading strategies to make meaning from a text. Perhaps it's time to take you back to your

Clarks school-shoe days and relive some of what young readers need to do on a daily basis.

– –

You think this reading thing is easy? Read this!

The man and woman had a row about how best to row the boat over the bumpy sea. They were shouting so much they almost missed the deer standing on the shore. It was such a dear sight to see. The deer was anxious, for sure, and then they saw why: there was a buck in the bushes. 'Does the doe know it is there?' the woman asked. 'I know that bucks do funny things when does are present.' And then the buck launched an attack. It tore at the doe's side and bolted. The woman saw the doe's tear and shed a tear. They pulled into the shore and tried to dress the tear. The man held the deer while the woman wound a bandage tightly around the wound. When they were done, the doe stood and fled.

– –

If you're a good reader, nothing in this paragraph will have taxed you, but I'm expecting you had to employ some reading strategies to get it right. I'm also betting you weren't even totally aware you were doing it.

* Did you read the first 'row' in the opening sentence and then read on to realise you had it wrong? If so, you would have mentally revised it in a split second, almost like an autocorrect, in order to make sense of the sentence.
* As an experienced reader, you would have had no problem coping with 'shore' and 'sure', 'deer' and 'dear', and 'sea' and 'see'. Or

the trickier sentences containing 'does', 'doe's and 'does' (plural of doe). But imagine what these would do to a child at the early stages of reading mastery?

* You may have had to read to the end to correct the sentence about the doe having a tear and the woman with a tear.

* And you certainly would have drawn on your knowledge of the various ways the word 'dress' can be used to make sense of 'They pulled into shore and tried to dress the tear.' But you can understand why a child who knows only that 'dress' is an item of clothing will struggle to read this sentence correctly. Knowledge of vocabulary helps readers make sense of what they read.

And these are just some of the pitfalls children need to negotiate when they're already knee-deep in trying to learn sound systems, sight words and more. Learning to read the English language is tough, of that there is no doubt. Everyone can learn to read it, though: of that there is also no doubt. It's all in the blend of ingredients and adjusting the measures of each to match individual needs.

But aren't humans built for learning to read?

The short answer is no. There have been lots of mixed messages about reading over the years; one is that learning to read is instinctive and intuitive – as natural as walking and talking. Believe me, it's not, although I can understand why many think it must be. Children learn to talk by living in a world where they hear words spoken; therefore, they'll learn to read via the same sort of osmosis technique, right? That sounds like it makes perfect sense, but it's wrong, and there's nothing natural at all about learning to read. Here's why.

🔅 FACT

Our brains are not wired for reading. They're wired for speaking.

If you're one of the lucky ones, your child might learn to read just by being immersed in a world of beautiful literature and quality reading material. Indeed, there is an enormous amount to be gained from this approach (more on this later) and it *is* one of those essential ingredients for learning to read, but it *isn't* the only ingredient. Using just this approach alone will not make a reader of *every* child.

It takes a combination of strategies for most children. Reading is such an autopilot thing for us that we can be lulled into thinking our brains must be hardwired for it. The fact is, from the beginning, humans have been oral communicators and oral storytellers, our brains wired for talking. As we've evolved, we've been speakers for tens of thousands of years longer than we have been readers and writers. In fact, humans have spent roughly only 8 per cent of their time writing and reading, and because of this, our brains have been configured for speech.

🔅 FACT

The first known examples of written language (writing that humans read) date back about only 5000 years – a tiny fraction of the 60,000 years that humans have spent using spoken language.

So, reading and writing are a relatively new thing for us, but what does this mean for our brains? A full scientific explanation on brain evolution could easily be a book in itself, and not one that I am qualified to write. Put simply for our purposes, it means that our brains haven't had enough time to evolve with a predisposition for literacy. We've been doing it for far too short a period for any major evolutionary brain developments to have taken place.

All this means is that we have no designated area in our brains for learning to read, and so we need to teach ourselves to read using areas of the brain developed for other tasks. We have to use what we've evolved with – the areas responsible for language, speech and visual processing. We repurpose these areas when we learn to read and that's why it doesn't come naturally. So, we have to teach a long-evolved old dog new tricks in order to do it, and some brains are more comfortable than others with learning new tricks and finding the quickest way of performing them.

Even when we've mastered the reading process and are competent readers, a 'reading centre' still doesn't just materialise or develop in our brains. That bit of brain evolution is going to take a while yet for all of us. Meanwhile, we have to work hard at acquiring our reading skills. To do this, we have to build the neural connections needed through successful instruction.

What are our brains doing when we learn to read?

Our brain is operating like a superhighway when we read. Lots of information must travel on these highways at the same time, and needs to flow at a speedy rate for it all to come together and work smoothly – without hitting any roadblocks along the way! In skilled readers, these superhighways have been built, and built well. Information can, therefore, travel so quickly and easily that the entire process takes less than half a second.

In children, whose highways are still being built, the process is slower and more labour-intensive. Here's what the process looks like and where it happens in the brain:

1. When the child sees a word, the visual part of their brain will receive it from the eyes and process it, just like any other visual stimulus. As this area recognises more and more words by sight, the faster the child will be able to read.

2. At the same time, another part of the child's brain will be busy working out what the word's spoken equivalent is, and it needs to get this right.

3. Yet another area will decode or sound out the word if it is unfamiliar.

4. A further area of the child's brain will be coming up with the word's meaning.

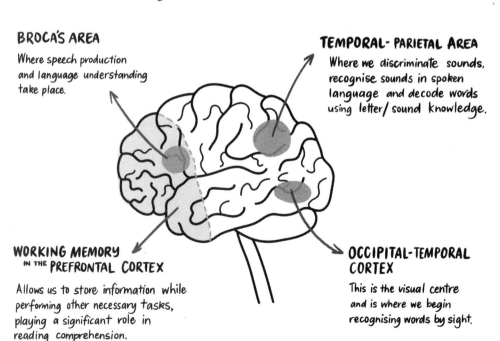

BROCA'S AREA
Where speech production and language understanding take place.

TEMPORAL- PARIETAL AREA
Where we discriminate sounds, recognise sounds in spoken language and decode words using letter/sound knowledge.

WORKING MEMORY IN THE **PREFRONTAL CORTEX**
Allows us to store information while performing other necessary tasks, playing a significant role in reading comprehension.

OCCIPITAL-TEMPORAL CORTEX
This is the visual centre and is where we begin recognising words by sight.

What happens in the brain when children struggle to read?

A struggling reader is not lazy – far from it! They are not stupid either. The danger is that they will believe they are if they don't progress or get the help they need before they become disengaged.

Children who are struggling readers and who don't get the intervention they need do not get better at reading, and will fall further and further behind.

Significant progress over the past two decades in the area of neuroscience has done much to clarify how we learn to read. Brain-imaging studies are finally shedding much-needed light on why some children struggle

Dyslexia

Dyslexic children struggle with knowing what sounds relate to which letters (decoding to read) and how to convert sounds to the correct written letters (spelling and writing). As a result, they have trouble reading single words. What is important to know is that this is a difference in how their brains work, not that there is something wrong with their intelligence or understanding. These children may struggle with decoding but not necessarily with comprehension and other language skills. Read a story aloud to them and they will love it, understand it, comprehend it and relate to it. We'll see more on this subject in the final chapter, 'Difficulty learning to read, write and spell'.

and others don't. It's still early days and it's not yet at a point where it could be used for diagnosis, but neuroscience is a powerful tool to complement the work of teachers, speech pathologists and specialist reading educators on how best to turn struggling readers into happy, confident ones.

Back roads rather than superhighways

Brain imaging is allowing doctors to identify the parts of the brain that are activated during the reading process. In many children with dyslexia, for example, several studies have confirmed that a high level of activation takes place in other areas of the brain, with much less activation in the areas that stronger readers use.[1] The brains of dyslexic children are completely capable but their superhighways are less developed or are underused. Rather, they tend to use the much slower neural back roads and country lanes to get to the same place.

These children are expending enormous amounts of energy doing it this way and it produces very little yield. They're working much harder and getting minimal gain for their pain. It's no wonder many become disengaged and are turned off by the whole reading thing. These children need to train their brains to use and develop pathways other than the ones they've been using.

To develop the reading superhighways that effective readers use, these children must activate and use these other areas again and again. And the way to do it is with specific, targeted and intensive reading instruction. Through this carefully controlled and consistent instruction, the patterns of brain activation in these children can be changed, causing an increase in their ability to learn to read. This subject is covered in more detail in the chapter titled 'Difficulty learning to read, write and spell'.

What do children need to know for their brains to get on with literacy?

There are seven key skills that early readers need a working knowledge of so they can get the whole reading and writing process happening in the relevant areas of the brain. I've summarised these on the following page.

How can you ensure the super skills happen smoothly for your Gen A child?

When the super skills work together smoothly and efficiently, children learn to read. However, it's a complicated, multi-layered task, this reading thing, and the acquisition of these skills is a journey and a process – a very individual one. But children are clever, eager, ready and certainly up for the task.

What is important is that they arrive at school ready. What takes place in the early years holds the key to this readiness: it is what will set them up to sail rather than fail, and in the next few chapters we will explore how to ensure your child is school-ready.

For Gen Alpha, the early years have become tricky. For the last decade, many young children have been part of an unintentional global experiment as the first generation to have access to devices and screens from the cradle, and it has turned things on their head. This and other changes are impacting on how literacy-ready they are when they arrive at school, and educators are seeing this play out in their literacy journeys.

So, let's unpack the ingredients – the seven steps that will allow the super skills to come together like a finely oiled machine and set our kids up to soar.

The super skills

1. **ALPHABETICAL AWARENESS:** this is the basic understanding that written words are made up of letters of the alphabet and are parts of spoken words.

2. **PHONOLOGICAL AWARENESS:** this is the ability to focus on the sounds of spoken language rather than their meaning – examples include hearing the rhyme patterns in a list of words, and in the sounds of rhythms that make up words.

3. **ENCODING:** this involves being able to translate speech sounds into the letters that represent those sounds – the sounding out of words to write them.

4. **LETTER AND SOUND KNOWLEDGE:** the understanding that the sounds they hear can be represented on paper using letters and blends of letters. The relationship between the sounds and the letters that represent them is fundamental for reading and is known as decoding.

5. **VOCABULARY:** this is a knowledge of the meaning of words and their uses. When children know the meaning of a word, they have a much better chance of being able to read it and make sense of it in a sentence.

6. **FLUENCY:** this is the ability to read text quickly, accurately and with appropriate expression. This happens when all the other components are so honed that a child does them automatically, freeing them up to access text as a competent reader.

7. **COMPREHENSION:** this is the endgame. When a reader can read, and understand and remember what it is that they've read, they've made it!

Takeaways from this chapter

* There is no one-size-fits-all when it comes to reading instruction.
* Our brains have not evolved for reading and writing. They are wired for speech. We repurpose areas of the brain to learn to read.
* To teach our brains to read, we must build the neural pathways (or superhighways). The way to do this is by activating those pathways consistently and regularly with quality reading instruction.

* There is much that can be done in the early years to ensure that the construction of these highways takes place. It is important for children to arrive at school brain-ready for learning to read.
* Every child needs to master the super skills. To do this, some may need more instruction in one area and less in others. All children need all seven in place to be successful, confident readers.

'Children are made readers on the laps of their parents'

- EMILY BUCHWALD

Step 1:
Talking their way to literacy

It is mid-winter and I'm sitting in a crowded surgery waiting room. It smells of wet woollen jumpers and feels overheated. I can almost see the germs multiplying in the stuffiness. I'm here to see the GP for a referral, and apart from one other man and his child, I'm the only one without a cold. As I rub some antibacterial sanitiser into my hands, I scan the room to see how many people might be ahead of me. What I see is a room filled with adults engrossed with their smartphones or devices.

I don't have a problem with this. I may even join them.

But just then, a toddler places a well-loved toy car in her carer's lap and babbles away with a big smile. I watch as the carer places the toy on the floor and pushes it along, his eyes never leaving his device and never a word escaping his lips. The child, unfazed, pushes the car under a chair and heads back to the toy basket. I watch her, amused as she selects and disregards items according to criteria known only to her. In no time, toys are strewn about the floor.

Just when I think she will find nothing of interest, she pulls out a strange-looking rabbit-robot. She turns, holds the toy up to show her carer, and says, 'De-da-owww,' finishing with a high-pitched squeal that makes me laugh out loud. Weirdly, I am the one who is rewarded with a reaction from her carer; a half smile, a slight shrug, and then it's back to his device.

I swallow the urge to say to this person, 'Your child is talking to you.' I swallow the urge to ask how he would have felt if I'd ignored him when he gave me that half-smile-shrug. I swallow the urge to point out that it takes two to talk. Of course, he could just be having a bad day or dealing with a serious situation on his device. Who am I to know or judge? But I struggle to squash the thought that this child's speech deserves a response.

Can talking really make a reader?

Oral language is one of the strongest foundations for learning to read. From birth to five years, talking and interacting is the most critical thing parents and carers can do to prepare children for learning to read at school. In 2002, a National Early Literacy Panel was formed in the USA to review the global scientific research on the development of early literacy skills in children aged zero to five. It took the panel six years to collate, examine and publish their findings. On oral language's role in learning to read, this was their finding:

🔦 FACT

A child's oral language and vocabulary are key early predictors of learning-to-read success. In turn, the less experience a child has with language and literacy, the more likely it is that he or she will have difficulty learning to read.

Tuning in rather than out in the early years

There has been much published about devices and screen-dependent children, but the research on screen-distracted parents and carers is just as compelling, and it's very real. The term 'continuous partial attention' was coined by technology expert Linda Stone more than twenty years ago and it's very different from multi-tasking.

Stone says that when we multi-task, our motivation is to be more efficient, more productive. When we multi-task, we usually combine several autopilot things at once that don't require much brain power: sort and fold the washing, talk on the phone and eat lunch. Continuous partial attention means exactly that: the scanning across several social media platforms, 'always on' and 'live' on the network at all times, and rarely fully present in anything. It consumes our brain power much more than multi-tasking because we are not on autopilot when we do it.

As adults, we have choices about how we manage our attention. We can choose to turn off technology in order to give full attention to others. And when it comes to children, like in most things, balance is the key. The occasional parental lapse in attention is normal and isn't going to damage a child who lives in a loving and responsive environment.

In fact, some developmental scientists suggest that some lapses in attention may even teach children patience and resilience.

However, research confirms that children suffer when they have to compete for their parents' full attention too much of the time, and their language acquisition often takes a big hit. This is because they're missing out on the quality face-to-face interaction they need. Inattention has always been around; constant online access has not, and Gen A are the first generation to compete with devices for their parents' or carers' attention.

I found it both heartening and heart-wrenching to learn recently that maternal and child health nurses now include instruction on the importance of talking to your child (and being fully present when you do so) in the arsenal of information that they send home with new parents. Who would've thought we'd have to remind humans of this seemingly fundamental thing? And it's not because the nurses think parents don't value talking: it's to make sure they are aware of the critical connection that talking to their baby plays in the development of oral language and, in turn, learning to read.

FACT

The more parents and carers speak with and to their babies and toddlers, the better these children will be at understanding speech and learning words.

Baby brains, babble and language-learning

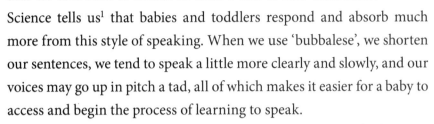

So yes, that baby babble is important, and even more so is that we talk back to babies in what I like to call 'bubbalese'. Science tells us[1] that babies and toddlers respond and absorb much more from this style of speaking. When we use 'bubbalese', we shorten our sentences, we tend to speak a little more clearly and slowly, and our voices may go up in pitch a tad, all of which makes it easier for a baby to access and begin the process of learning to speak.

And the good news is that babies' brains are hardwired for learning language. It's instinctive and inbuilt from the get-go, which is why children make language learning look so easy to us adults. Too bad it isn't the same for learning to read and write!

For our part, all we have to do is talk with them, sing with them and read aloud to them. In fact, scientific research tells us that at least ten days before the birth, a child begins recognising the sounds of its mother's language and, once they are born, they will recognise a song or lullaby that was sung to them while in the womb. Oral language development really does start this early.

The science of how babies learn to speak

Advances in neuroscience and brain imaging have meant that our understanding of how the brain works has also advanced, and revealed that a baby's brain is pretty amazing!

* Babies are born with billions of brain cells.
* They come complete with almost all the brain cells they will ever have.
* Babies form more than one million brain connections every second in response to experiences, and the quality of those experiences really matters.

* It's the quality of a baby's relationships that has a major influence on how brain connections take place and on how strong those connections are.
* The early years are the most active period for establishing brain connections.

So, what exactly are brain connections and how do they form?

Brain cells make connections with other brain cells. That point of connection is called a synapse. Hardwiring in the brain occurs when these connections are stimulated with repeated use. Brain-imaging technology confirms that this repeated stimulation or activation allows signals to be transmitted quickly, and it is this that creates efficient, accurate and permanent neural pathways.

The bad news is that brain imaging also confirms that it's a use-it-or-lose it arrangement. Unused connections that don't get stimulated repeatedly, degenerate and atrophy in a process called pruning.

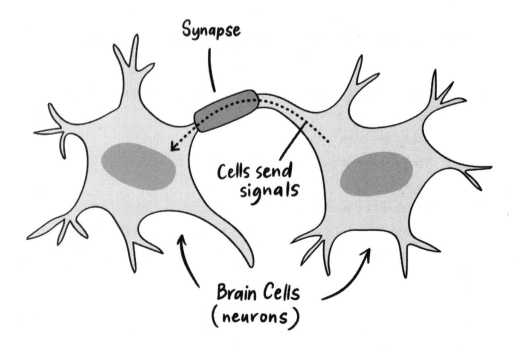

Synapse

Cells send signals

Brain Cells (neurons)

Given that the early years are the most active for forming brain connections, and that babies' brains are hardwired for learning oral language, parents and carers need to maximise this time. They do this by engaging their children in what developmental researchers call 'contingent reciprocity' and immersing them in a language-rich environment. The Center on the Developing Child at Harvard University's work on brain architecture, represented in this diagram, shows that the brain is quicker at forming connections at a younger age.

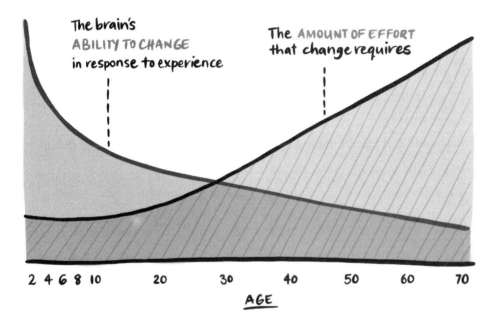

Contingent recip– what?

Contingent reciprocity is a big name for a straightforward concept. Put simply, it is a back-and-forth appropriate engagement with a baby.

When babies babble, cry or use facial expressions or gestures, we respond to them with appropriate responses – we use eye contact, words, facial expressions, hugs. When we do this again and again, connections are made and strengthened in the area of a child's brain responsible

31

for communication and social skills. Healthy brain connections are built on appropriate responses. If the adult's responses aren't the right match for the stimulus – an angry response when the baby is seeking a smile or reassurance, or simply no response at all – healthy brain wiring will suffer.

Parents and carers can use the following 'TALK' activity over and over as children grow.

T Tune in to the child's facial expressions and body movement. Are they pointing or looking at something?

A Acknowledge their communication with sounds, words, facial expressions or a hug. Let them know you are focusing on the same thing. Imitate their babble back to them.

L Label what they give you or what they see, feel, hear or do. Giving a name to what they're focusing on will help them begin to make those important language connections in their brains.

K Keep the back and forth going. Take turns speaking and waiting for them to respond. These are the foundations of dialogue and conversation!

FACT

Gaps in children's language and vocabulary first appear between eighteen months to two years. Children whose parents speak to them more often know many more words by the age of two; by the age of three, some children have vocabularies two to three times larger than others. Those with much smaller vocabularies arrive at school significantly behind their peers and will struggle or be slower to learn to read.[2]

From birth to five years really is the top time for learning language. While learning and language acquisition are occurring throughout development, scientists now know that a child's early years are optimal brain-development periods for learning language. Here they are at a glance.

0–6 months: Initially babies hear the sound of all languages, but by six months they only recognise sounds in their native language – sounds they have heard repeated over and over. They start trying to make the same sounds you make and begin learning the mouth movements that go with different sounds.

6–12 months: They begin to play with sounds and recognise a few simple words. They will use their bodies to communicate with us, such as by pointing.

12–24 months: This is the period when a child's brain lays down synaptic connections for words and corresponding objects or images. They will learn the words used consistently for a particular object, such as 'bottle'. By the end of this period, they can follow directions and understand more of what you are saying. Many will have built a vocabulary of between 200–300 words.

24–36 months: This is the year children's language will really take off. Often, vocabulary will increase to more than a thousand words. They begin to ask questions, string words together and construct sentences. More and more pretend play provides opportunity to deepen the richness of the language they are exposed to through conversation, books, songs and incidental play.

3–5 years: Children continue to expand their vocabulary. They comprehend longer and more complex sentences, and they lengthen their own sentences. They begin to follow others' conversations. They play with lots of new and wonderful words and can sit for longer periods enjoying and comprehending stories read aloud to them. This is the period where comprehension of words, sentences and more complex stories grows in leaps and bounds.

Making it count is easy!

So we've seen that a parent's or carer's interactions are the key to a child's development of language. But let's face it, if we did it all day, every day, when would we have time to do everything else?

The great news is that everyday activities provide loads of opportunities for language development. If you talk with your child as you bath them, feed them, play with them and dress them you'll have it covered. Pick your moments and make them count. Here are some tips to maximise impact:

* Let children hear words over and over. Remember, they'll need to hear a word at least 250 times to learn it![3]
* Make sure that everyone who is important and involved in caring for a child is on board with the TALK strategy, and are talking and interacting with the child as they grow.
* As they grow, try to extend their speech and vocabulary by repeating what they've said, then adding just a bit more. Encourage them to tell you more. Ask questions about what they've said: 'Was the dog white or brown?'

Suggestions for everyday language-learning activities

Try to incorporate some of these spoken activities into your child's day:

* Do lots of TALK sessions.
* Allow your baby to eavesdrop on your adult conversations.

* Repeat the sounds your baby makes and make up new ones for them to try.
* Play object-naming games.
* Play mirror games labelling body features, facial expressions and actions.
* Converse with them about what they will wear each day.
* Include them in the packing of a lunchbox, labelling items as you go.
* Sing along to nursery rhymes and songs, doing any corresponding actions.
* Discuss your everyday activities, such as preparing a meal or getting dressed.
* Play games like 'I Spy' and memory games like 'I went shopping and bought . . .'
* Play rhyming word games.
* Use their pretend-play moments for conversation: be the other person on the end of the toy phone, be the other doll going to the shops.
* Build on their speech when you respond, for example, 'Dog!' 'Yes, it's a white fluffy dog, isn't it?'
* Ask questions and urge them to follow directions.
* Sing lots of nursery rhymes together.
* Let them mix with children of varying ages. They will pick up so much from other children.

Tips for cuddling up with a book for language development

At a very young age:

* Black-and-white books are good for younger babies from birth to six months. Newborns have quite blurred eyesight and the crisp contrasts of black and white are much easier for them to see.

* Once they move through the black-and-white stage, show them books that have photos of babies and that use bright colours.
* Vinyl, fabric and board books are great at this age.
* Share board books with textures for feeling and touching.
* Always start at the front of the book and share just a few pages. That's enough!

From nine months on:

* Read lift-the flap books and help them explore them using word/picture correspondence.
* Share books with rhyme, repetition and patterns.
* Topics about their everyday experiences will resonate: family, play, bathtime, colours, bedtime.
* Read animal books and make the noises with them.
* Share books with songs, nursery rhymes and early concepts such as numbers, shapes, vehicles.
* Watch digital read-aloud videos of books together.
* As they grow, share books with rich language, vivid worlds and engaging storylines.

Sharing books over and over with your child is excellent for their language development and allows them to become familiar enough with books to move into the driver's seat from as young as twelve months:

* When they're old enough, let them choose the book they want to read with you.
* Let them turn the pages, point to things and signal when they are ready for the next page.
* Let them approximate reading by telling you the story with their baby babble or words.

* If you are reading aloud, stop and encourage them to supply what comes next.
* Invite them to point to and name the things they see.
* Ask questions about the object, the illustrations, the story.
* Encourage them to point to the words as they tell you the story.

A few of these simple activities every day will mean that by the time your child arrives at school at around age five, they will be ready to learn to read and will possess a healthy vocabulary and strong understanding of language, ensuring their reading journey will be that much easier.

> *'Reading comprehension depends on language abilities that have been developing since birth . . . [and the] understanding of words and their interrelationships in and across individual sentences.'*[4]
>
> **– WALTER KINTSCH & EILEEN KINTSCH**

On comprehension

Your understanding of a sentence may differ from your child's as they learn to navigate our language, phrasing, idioms and more. When in doubt, ask a few questions to check their understanding. When sharing books, discuss the incidents in the text together and ask questions about what happened. You'll soon know if they're getting the gist or not.

I still laugh when I think of my son Tim at age four. He had a spectacular vocabulary and a voracious love of literature. Here are two conversations with him at this age that have gone down in our family's store of treasured stories. Weirdly, they're both from frazzled car trips!

I'm negotiating horrid Sydney traffic. Tim and his elder sister Sarah are in the back of the car, both restless. They're eager to see their grandmother, whom I've arranged to pick up outside a landmark in the city before we drive on to Balmoral. I explain that we are going to pick up Grandma outside a big building and then head on for a swim and lunch.

At this, Tim goes quiet. I take a quick glance in the rear-view mirror and can tell his little mind is ticking away. He asks me to tell him what is going to happen again. And I do. This time, he starts to cry. He becomes really distressed, but I can't think what could be wrong. I try to find a spot to pull over. It turns out that he's crying and upset about Grandma – he can't pick her up because she's too big, and then she won't be able to come to Balmoral with us, and the day will be ruined, and it is all his fault.

Tim genuinely heard 'picking up' Grandma in the literal sense, and he remained a very literal child through his primary-school years. Being aware of this helped a great deal, and to be completely honest, until then I hadn't really thought about our language and children's literal comprehension as they master it. Tim taught me this, and I'm forever grateful. Yet it didn't take him long to master language so well that he could play with it, manipulate it to his advantage and have fun with it.

It is a year later; same car, same children, one year older. They are very close in age and are experts at knowing how to torment each other. It's a stinking hot day and they're ramping the torment up to a new level in the back seat. It's stretching my patience. I'm close to snapping when I see the middle seatbelt buckle fly in the direction of Sarah's face. A high-pitched scream ensues. We pull over so I can clean up the mess of a bloody nose, and I lose it.

Me: Enough! Can you just please stay apart?

Tim: But if we stay apart, we'll fall to pieces.

And the twitch of a smile at the corners of his mouth as he says this is all it takes. I try like the best of us to smother my amusement and maintain my disciplinarian mode, but it's hopeless. I'm laughing, and the anger has dissipated because I know his play on my words is just so darn clever, and I can tell he has the visual of him and Sarah falling to pieces flicking like a cartoon before his eyes. I think to myself, 'Don't squash this skill. He may end up using it when he is older.'

And sure enough, now Tim plays with words and pictures for a living.

A note on devices and speech development

Studies have shown that the more time children between six months and two years spend on devices such as smartphones, tablets, electronic games and screens, the more likely they are to experience speech delays. Video-chatting is another matter, though. This is a great way to get them talking.[5]

Some oral-language games

Homemade family talk books

This is where you get to use all those fabulous photos you snap of your children on your devices! Print them and staple them together to make family talk books. Once you've created a book, share it with your child and encourage them to tell you what they're doing in each of the photos. These books will generate loads of fabulous discussion and become some of your most treasured keepsakes from their childhood. And they're cheap and easy to create.

You can snap categories of photos like the ones suggested in the list below over several weeks and then collate them. As children grow, you can make more complex books and even storybooks including their playmates! Later, you can help them write their own stories to match the pictures. The sky is the limit with homemade books, and they are a wonderful record of your child's early years.

Here are some ideas to get you started:

* Take photos of your child exploring at the park and other places.
* Photograph your child eating different foods/meals.
* Capture your child doing self-care activities such as sleeping, brushing their teeth, washing their hands.
* 'What am I wearing?' Photograph your child in different sets of clothes.
* Photograph your child doing an activity such as cooking, and document every stage. It could be something as simple as making jelly!

The mirror game

Stand together in front of a mirror, asking your child questions like: *Can you find your nose? Can you find your hair?*

Don't stop there. Change it around and go through as many categories as you can think of. Try showing emotions on faces: *Can you make a happy face?* Try things you can touch: *Can you touch your shirt?*

Play the Hokey Pokey with variations

Sing the Hokey Pokey song together or play an appropriate version from *Play School* or YouTube. This song is great for teaching body parts, but you can also play it with objects.

Once you've done the traditional verses for body parts –

You put your right hand in,
You put your right hand out,
You put your right hand in,
And you shake it all about!
You do the Hokey Pokey and you turn around,
That's what it's all about!

– try substituting body parts with things like your child's teddy, truck, ball or pyjamas!

Name two things

You can play this game with any category that's familiar to your child. *Let's name two toys. Let's name two things we like to eat. Let's name two items in your bedroom* (or other room in the home). As they grow, try increasing it to five and then ten things, and expand your categories to become more challenging.

Feely bags

Use any bag that can't be seen through. With younger children, place one very familiar item in the bag. Ask them to feel what's inside the bag and tell you what they think it is. Ask them to use any word they have to describe it. You might like to prompt: *Is it hard? Is it soft?*

As they grow, you can ask them more questions to encourage a description of the item and how they guessed what it was. You can add more items to the bag for older children to increase the challenge.

Nursery rhyme and verse play

Sing traditional nursery rhymes together. Once your child is familiar with them, make up your own versions. Here are two to start you off. Be as creative as you like!

This little piggy ate honey on toast,
This little piggy had cheese,
This little piggy ate avocado,
This little piggy had milk,
This little piggy went wee, wee, wee,
All the way home.

Five little puppies jumping on the bed,
One rolled off and bumped his head,
Four little puppies crawling on the bed,
One rolled off and bumped her head,
Three little puppies sleeping on the bed,
One rolled off and bumped his head,
Two little puppies eating on the bed,
One rolled off and bumped her head,
One little puppy laughing on the bed,
He rolled off and bumped his head.

Scavenger hunt

You can play this in any room in the home. For younger children, start with just one item and ask them to find it and bring it to you. As they grow, have them think up the items and name them instead of bring them to you. Increase the number of items to make it more challenging.

In the bedroom, I can find a blanket, a book and a pillow.
In the kitchen, I can find a cup, some coffee and a fridge.

I spy

Traditionally played as a letter/sound game *(I spy with my little eye something beginning with b)*, this game can be modified for children up to four years old by choosing categories instead of letters. When you do begin to play this with older children using letters, be sure to start with the sound for the letters first! Here are some suggestions:

Colours: *I spy with my little eye something yellow.*
Groups of objects: *I spy with my little eye something in the park.*
Clothing: *I spy with my little eye something I can wear.*

Colour days

This game will help your child learn colours and gain a sense of the days in the week. To play, make each day of the week a particular colour. If Monday is blue, let your child find one (or more, depending on what they have) blue item of clothing to wear. Choose a different colour for each of the seven days of the week. Soon they'll be telling you what colour day it is, so get your own wardrobe sorted as well before you start!

Make me a rhyme

All these games help to prepare your child for acquiring the super skills easily, but this one is particularly invaluable for the second super skill: phonological awareness, or hearing the sounds and patterns in words.

To play, start with a word, then add another rhyming word to it. Encourage your child to help you build a list. Don't worry if their words are nonsense words; it doesn't matter, as long as they rhyme. Start with short lists of two and three words, and as children grow, increase the length of the word lists. At this stage, as long as the rhyme works, don't worry about the spellings. This is all about hearing the sound patterns in spoken language.

Here is an example:

tree

tea

see

flea

three

me

fee-fee

- -

For my top book recommendations to get children talking
and app suggestions to encourage oral literacy,
head over to the 7 Steps section of my website.

- -

Takeaways from this chapter

* Consider how much your child competes for your undivided attention and ensure a balance, even if it means switching off devices for periods of time.
* Maximise time for face-to-face interaction in the very early years.
* Allow plenty of opportunity to hear language spoken. Immerse your child in the sounds of their native tongue.

* No matter their age or vocabulary development, treat children as little conversationalists – even if they have no words yet! Observe all the conversational courtesies you would like to receive: they will learn from your modelling of this.
* Sing songs and recite and act out nursery rhymes together.
* Spend time associating people and objects with words: 'I'm Mumma. This is a cup.'
* Read aloud from books, books and more books, pointing to the illustrations as you do.
* Allow them to tell you a story, using their babble, their words or their sentences.
* As they grow, encourage them to talk with other children of mixed ages. It will help expand their vocabulary and their conversation skills.
* Tightly limit exposure to devices between the ages of six months and two years.
* And remember, you and your child's primary carers are the most important factor in your child's oral language learning. So, have those conversations, sing those songs, read those books aloud, question, listen, respond appropriately, and know that all you do, all you say, all your interactions are setting them up for a smoother learning-to-read ride when they start school.

'Oh magic hour,
when a child first
knows she can
read printed words.'

-BETTY SMITH

Step 2:
Reading their way to literacy

Isabella is just eighteen months old when she sits on my rug to 'read' her way through my collection of picture books. She selects a well-loved thirty-year-old copy of Pamela Allen's *Who Sank the Boat?* She's not talking as such yet; she just has the classic few words you'd expect at this age, but she has the intonation and gist of the story in the noises she makes, and I know it won't be long before they turn into perfectly formed words.

I watch as she opens the cover and turns the title page – right hand to top-right corner and the page is turned relatively smoothly. No mean feat for such young hands. She takes in the double-page illustration and then her fingers move from left to right along the line of words. As they do, her little voice says, 'Er, er, er, er-ermmm,' with an intonation that conveys, 'Where are they all going?' She continues right to the end of the book in this fashion; the page-turning, the eyes greedily taking in the illustrations, the fingers pointing out the words from left to right accompanied by her 'storytelling'.

Somebody is doing a sensational job of helping this child read her way to literacy. I know who the somebodies are, given I'm babysitting their child, and I silently congratulate and cheer them on wholeheartedly!

A year and a bit later, same child, same rug, almost the same pile of books. She is unaware that I'm in the kitchen listening as she opens Graeme Base's *The Sign of the Seahorse*. It was my son's favourite for a while when he was about eight years old. I hear a gasp as she takes in the stunning artwork of the underwater world and its inhabitants, and then she starts 'reading' in her own little way.

'Some aminals are quiet,' she says for the first double-page spread, whispering the word 'quiet'. Right hand turns the page at the top-right corner. 'And some aminals are LOUD!' – 'loud' shouted as loudly as she can.

She turns to the next page. 'Some aminals are sad and some are glad. But some are BAD!' The last word is also shouted and she feigns fright.

This child is melting my heart! Of course, her version of the story doesn't match the text, but it's a pretty awesome match for the illustrations. She continues her innovation on this text to the end and immediately starts over. What a thing to watch!

Isabella is going to read her way to literacy. By the time she starts school, she will have acquired a wealth of knowledge about the reading process that will help her on her literacy journey. Indeed, at two and a half, I can already see that she understands several fundamental things, all gained from adults sharing books with her from birth.

Isabella knows:

* that books are to be explored, enjoyed and loved – between the covers, they hold wonderful stories and interesting information
* how to hold a book the right way, and how to gather information from the cover on what the book might be about
* how to gently turn the pages, one at a time
* that there is a special relationship in picture books between the illustrations and the black squiggles running in a line that accompanies them – that the lines of text tell the story and that the illustrations support this and enrich the story process
* that words on a page represent speech and thought, and so these words can be read to tell the story
* that reading English is a process that goes from left to right
* that each group of black squiggles, bunched together with a tiny break before the next word starts, represents a spoken word
* about the patterns that might be found in stories – Isabella's imitation of the use of repetition to introduce new information is evident in her storytelling about the animals.
* some phonological awareness as she gets a rhythm going in her story, and produces three rhyming words. Truly brilliant!

That's a heck of a lot of knowledge to have garnered about reading by the young age of two and a half, all learnt from watching her role models as they share books with her. And all the while, this book-sharing continues to build and extend her vocabulary.

Isabella is busy conquering two of the super skills: phonological awareness and vocabulary. You could also argue that she is at the early stages of super skill number one: alphabetical awareness. While she is not yet exhibiting the knowledge that written words are made up of letters of the alphabet, she knows the precursor to this: that written words represent speech. This child is well on the way in her literacy acquisition journey, and it's a miraculous thing to witness.

I originally promised myself that I wouldn't write much about reading aloud and sharing books with your child from birth, because this is written about and shared so much now. I'm constantly being told that these days *everyone* knows about the importance of books in the early years. Moreover, there is so much more critical information that I want this book to address.

However, I was surprised to discover in a recent in-depth study on reading that 53 per cent of parents with children aged zero to five who were surveyed had not received the advice that children should be read aloud to from birth. That's an alarming statistic for a movement that has been going since at least the early 1980s! So, I will join the ranks that continue to get this message out.

A precious gift of joy

There are no rules about sharing books with your child; it's as individual as the people in your family. But if I had to make one rule, it would be this: in their early years, make it as special and as pleasurable for your child as you can. It's all about them having fun and finding books a positive thing: it's not about explicit teaching. There's plenty of time for that in the future.

For now, what's most important is instilling a love of books, where there is nothing but fun and enjoyment to be had; no blood, sweat and tears trying to read words and get things right, no dreary boredom that will disengage them, no effort on their part (or yours for that matter!) at all. Pure, positive interactions with books on the lap of a loved one trumps all in these early years. If you can manage this, then you will be giving them the most precious gift of all. A child who grows loving books and has nothing to fear from them will confidently take on the challenge of learning to read when the time comes – and with a much greater rate of success.

In their own words is gold!

Isabella's little cousin, Ellie, is twenty months old as I write this. I'm known as Lou-Lou to the family and recently she's begun to say my name. She calls me Yow-Yoo, and I think it's the most outrageously exciting and adorable thing. Her parents sent me a little video of her saying it. I have watched that video so many times I've lost count, and I've shown it to anyone and everyone.

The point I want to make about this is that I would never, ever think to tell her that Yow-Yoo is not correct and that my name is actually Lou-Lou. Rather, I lap up her attempt at my name and reward her with the biggest smiles, hugs and noises of delight.

Likewise, when Isabella was three and happily 'reading' Rod Campbell's *Dear Zoo* – a book that had been read to her enough that she was familiar with its text pattern – she read:

They gave me a giraffe but he was too big so I put him back.

The text actually read:

So they sent me a giraffe. He was too tall. I sent him back.

I would not have dreamt of correcting this either. I accepted Isabella's version as she turned the pages and kept going in this pattern, because this approximating, or storytelling in her own words, is an important stepping stone to learning to read. Just as I delighted in Ellie's approximation of my name, I celebrated Isabella's approximation of *Dear Zoo*. She was 'reading', and doing a mighty fine job of it too!

A child who is allowed to explore the world of books on their own terms like this is acquiring skills that will impact their later success in learning to read. Of that there is no doubt. This is not the time for admonishing and correcting so that every word 'read' is done so accurately. It's a time for praise and celebration. Video their early attempts at reading. Enjoy them, because like all stages and milestones in littlies, these will be gone in the blink of an eye.

What does your child stand to gain?

That reading aloud and sharing books from a very young age promotes language development and other early literacy skills is well-documented and irrefutable. Children exposed to books from birth receive a long-lasting literacy boost that gives them a headstart when they arrive at school. Children who miss out on this will find it hard to catch up and close the gap.

☀️ FACT

Reading aloud, shared reading and interactive talking in the early years (from birth to five) are the most significant activities for building the knowledge necessary for children to learn to read when they start school.

Parents, grandparents and anyone else who plays a key role in your child's life can help your child enjoy these benefits and get the much-needed boost they deserve.

This table shows the invaluable knowledge and skills a child can acquire just from adults sharing books with them in an enjoyable and fun way.

Sharing books between 0–12 months:

* creates a special bond between parents and children
* exposes children to the sounds and words of language
* develops a growing awareness that books are just as important and valuable as toys
* allows exploration of books and how they work – opening covers and turning pages of board books, cloth books and foam bath books
* enhances listening skills
* activates areas of the brain in readiness for learning to read.

Sharing books between 1–3 years also:

* fosters a love of reading
* develops appropriate book-handling skills: opening the cover, turning pages, starting at the beginning and progressing to the end
* develops understanding that print represents spoken words
* exposes children to the written language in books, which is different to how we speak

* fosters an awareness that in the English language print is read from left to right
* encourages basic understanding of story structure: a beginning, middle and end
* develops recognition of story patterns: predictable repetition, rhyming, rhythm of stories
* enhances understanding that print and illustrations work together to tell a story
* builds and enriches vocabulary.

Sharing books between 3–5 years also:

* gives them basic phonological and alphabet knowledge: that letters make up words, that sounds can be represented by these letters, sensitivity to rhyming words and words that start with the same letter or end with the same letter
* introduces a wide variety of experiences, adventures and worlds, and can also reflect a familiar world – visits to the doctor, bedtime, bathtime, routines, play, starting preschool or school
* fires up the imagination
* helps with problem-solving skills
* develops social and emotional skills.

And it's not just about their brains, it's about their hearts too!

Cuddling with a child to share a book is a special moment, for the adult as well as the child. Sitting in the lap of someone who loves them, having that person all to themselves for those few precious minutes, makes a child feel loved, happy and safe. This goes way beyond just the building of their literacy skills. It helps develop their thinking skills and their ability to understand and empathise with others, and builds positive and constructive relationships.

Sharing for maximum gain

That's a lot of gain to be had from a bit of book-sharing. But how much book-sharing does it take? To be honest, I've heard all sorts of things – from a minimum of fifteen minutes every day to three full books every day. I've read articles about creating special, irresistible spaces to be exclusively used for reading up to five books at bedtime on a regular basis.

While all these recommendations sound wonderful, they aren't always achievable. Some people don't even feel comfortable reading aloud for various reasons, and I have some tips to help with that later in this chapter.

So, let's be realistic here; lives are busy, there is much to juggle, and as parents we already carry enough guilt. This book hasn't been written to dump more guilt on the pile. I know that some days you'll be too tired to read a few books before sleeptime. That some days go totally pear-shaped and it's all you can do to make it to the end of them without unravelling. Don't beat yourself up if a day goes by and you haven't shared a book with your child.

Remember that any exposure is good exposure. If you have a day where you manage to carve out ten minutes, great. If not, grab what you can where and when you can; one or two minutes when you're standing in line at the supermarket, five minutes while you wait in the doctor's surgery, a bath book while they're in the bath as a captive audience. It all counts. And no, you don't have to have a special reading nook that rivals the best of them on Pinterest or Instagram!

Below I've shared some tips by age to help you get the maximum bang for your book, but my biggest tip, no matter the age of the child, is this: let them run the show!

Not every child will sit, snuggled up, every time *you've* carved out a moment in your busy day to read with them. Some babies will just want to chew the book. Others will want to turn it over and over, or want to open and shut it. This is all valuable book-exploration experience. Toddlers may only want to read a few pages and stop. Let them. Don't try to keep them at it beyond their interest or attention span. You don't have to read the whole book with them – not at any age if they're not up for it. Nor do you have to read every book to them word for word.

Tips for reading with babies 0–12 months

* Choose durable books that won't tear easily and are chew-proof: board books, stiff-card books, cloth books, vinyl books that are waterproof and will wipe clean.

* Don't stress if your baby just wants to handle and even chew books. Book-handling is an important part of the process.

* Choose books with large, simple black and white images for very young babies.

* As they get bigger, choose books with bright colours and contrasting backgrounds; books with photos of faces, babies and toddlers; wordless picture books filled with familiar objects babies will recognise.

* Choose books with one-word labels or very short simple text. Nursery rhymes and illustrated songs are perfect for this age group.

* Give them books with different textures so that they can hear, see and feel them.
* When sharing books, it's best to hold books about 30cm away from babies' eyes.

Tips for reading with toddlers

* One or two minutes at a time is plenty. If they're happy to stay longer, make the most of it, but let them dictate the duration. Don't worry if they up and run off! If you keep reading, they'll listen and may well come and go.
* Board books, lift-the-flap books, books with sounds, nonfiction books, picture books and concept books are all excellent for this age group.
* Choose books with simple, clear illustrations that they can easily identify.
* Show them the cover and talk about it.
* Tell them what the book is about by reading the back-cover blurb with them.
* Encourage them to turn the pages.
* Don't worry if they skip pages.
* Don't feel you have to read a story word for word. Use your own words and try to make the story as relatable and personal as you can.
* Choose simple books with a beat, rhythm and rhyme to them.
* Short punchy text is useful.
* Run your finger along the words as you read them.
* Point to the pictures and discuss them.
* Point to the words or labels of pictures and ask your toddler to supply words.
* Ask simple questions about the pictures.

Tips for reading with preschoolers

* Let them choose the books they'd like to borrow from the library or buy from the bookstore with your guidance and support.

* Books with predictable, repetitive patterns work well and they'll most likely ask for them again. Likewise, stories that rhyme and have a rhythm to them will appeal to your preschooler. Have them clap or sing along to the rhythm.

* Look for books on topics that you know interest your child.

* Choose stories that have a clear beginning, middle and end – nothing overly complicated.

* Simplify the story or just talk about the pictures if your child isn't interested in listening to the whole story at first. You still don't have to read every page if they don't want you to.

* Let them be in the driver's seat, even if you're the one reading: let them hold the book and turn the pages, and read aloud the story at their pace. Remember, you don't have to finish the book in one sitting – you don't have to finish it at all.

* Furthermore, let them take the wheel if you're not reading. Some children want to flip through books quickly, while some will look at one or two pages, close the book and walk away. Others will want to look at the entire book again and again. It's all okay.

* On the first read-through, provide time on each page for your child to do or say something. At a new page, give them time to look at the illustrations, to point something out to you if they wish, to talk to you about what they see. Try not to ask questions or point things out during a first read. You can do all that on the second read.

* Make the story come alive using different voices for the characters.
* On a second read, ask questions about the events in the story.
* In books with predictable patterns or repetitions, encourage your preschooler to finish the sentence or supply words.
* With familiar books, let them 'read' the story to you in their own way, using their own words, and encourage them to run their finger along the words as they do. Don't worry that what they say and what they point to don't match.
* Encourage them to tell you about the illustrations.

What to avoid

Books with few illustrations won't hold your young reader's attention and they'll find it harder to follow the story. They will also find lengthy, complicated stories taxing.

If you can, avoid using electronic books at this stage. Children learn more from paper books, and the buttons and game elements of ebooks tend to distract them from the story. There's something incredibly important about learning to physically turn the pages of a printed book, to examine the covers, to point to the words and illustrations as they were meant to appear; to know the worth of a book without needing gadgetry to entertain.

> *'The electronic format is a less efficient means of supporting internalisation of story content. The many attractive options of electronic books seems to divert children's attention from text and number of readings of the text.'*[1]
>
> **– MARIA DE JONG & ADRIANA BUS**

Electronic vs paper books

Kindergarten children aged 4–6 took part in a study to determine what differences were observed when reading a traditional paper book as opposed to reading an electronic e-book. The key findings showed that children who read electronic books at this age yielded very different results to children who read traditional books. They found that children reading hard-copy books:

* understood the content more thoroughly
* could recall and pronounce more words from the story.

And where children read ebooks with extra interactive features, they found that:

* children spent almost half the time playing games and exploring features unrelated to reading
* many pages were loaded without the text being read by the computer, with most children only rarely activating the read-aloud option.[2]

Reading aloud with primary-school children, tweens and even teens!

Although this chapter focuses on the importance of reading aloud to children in the early years before they start school, I feel it's worth mentioning here the benefits of continuing to read aloud through these older years. Of course, it's not something you need to do all the time like when they're little, but there is a reason why teachers still read aloud to classes right through to high school, and you can enhance these benefits by adding to their efforts at home. Here are some of the big reasons why you should keep reading aloud, no matter the age, along with a few tips for keeping them reading. More about reading and the school-aged child can be found in the last three chapters.

'A child's reading level doesn't catch up to their listening level until eighth grade.'[3]

– JIM TRELEASE

Why you should keep reading aloud for as long as possible

* For the sheer pleasure of it! It's a fact, children of all ages love to be read to – to have you all to themselves sharing something special together. And don't just take it from me. In a recent survey, older children made themselves very clear on this with 83 per cent of them stating that being read to was something they either loved or liked a lot. Yet only 17 per cent of the parents in the same study said they read aloud to their children after the age of eight. And if you think your tween or teen is not interested in being read to, start reading something aloud they'd enjoy to someone else in the home. You'll reel them in and have them sitting down and listening in no time!

* Reading aloud to your child allows them to comprehend, access and enjoy stories and information that are a bit too hard for them to read on their own. This expands their vocabulary and increases their literacy skills and knowledge of their world.

* It improves their listening skills.

* It's a great doorway to discussing difficult topics and problems your child might be facing. Reading aloud books that show characters struggling through issues such as exclusion, bullying,

racism, gender bias and so much more allows you to explore these issues from a position that's not quite as confronting – it's one step removed. What's more, seeing characters who are vulnerable, who are up against it but don't give up, who make poor choices and grow as a result also gives your child opportunity to empathise, to understand a difficult situation from another perspective, and to take their discoveries into their own lives and apply them.

* It brings back the magic of reading! Think about it – your child has just spent three or four years doing the hard slog of actually learning to read. Sure, they might be competent readers now, but chances are they see reading as that thing that had to be conquered and something to be tested and marked on. So many parents tell me that they worry because their child has gone off reading and that they wish they'd get back into it. When I ask how old they are, more often than not they're in about Year 4 or 5. And I think, yep, they've trudged their way through all the heavy reading and spelling rules and they've made it. But somewhere along the way, all the reading of readers to parents, carers, helpers and teachers, all the analysing texts in class, has replaced the wonderful 'being read to' moments. They've forgotten that there are sensational reads to be had, and they've lost sight of the sheer joy of getting totally lost in a book for the pure pleasure of it. Reading aloud to your older child will reignite this love and ensure they go on to be readers for life.

* It's your way of telling them that reading is a worthwhile activity to be valued, and that in the tween- and teen-busy world of technology and television, extracurricular and social pressures,

the gentle balm of words and story-sharing can soothe, comfort, recharge and use different parts of their brain and imagination.

* Even at these ages, there's nothing better than a good reader modelling the process of reading. All children learn a lot simply from observing, following on as you read aloud and just listening to how you read. As you read, pause to recap events in a story; make judgements about characters' motives, actions and dilemmas.

* Reading from a wide variety of genres, authors and types of texts will broaden their horizons. It can make genres your child might not usually chose more accessible for them. Often children get stuck on familiar styles.

* This point is a tip for those who have fidgety, easily distracted children – give them something to do with their hands. Squeezy toys and balls, anything it takes. Often their concentration improves when their hands are busy with something they can do on autopilot.[4]

* Even in older children who can read, reading aloud contributes significantly to their literacy success. They'll be better writers, better speakers, better listeners and better thinkers.

The best of the best read-aloud techniques

There are no hard and fast rules for sharing books with your child. In the early years, it's all about opportunity and enjoyment, and the tips on pages 58–63 will guide you. As your child grows and moves through primary school, you may want to use a more targeted approach to reading books together, particularly when dealing with readers that the school may send home with your child. Here are some popular methods used in classrooms that have been found to yield good results. You may come across varying names for these approaches and I'm using the ones that I know, but the reading methods will be the same.

Parent-directed shared reading

In parent-directed shared reading, the adult reads the book aloud. You can begin by discussing the cover and predicting what the book might be about. Then read the story to your child without interruption. On the second read-through, pause as you go to ask questions about the story and discuss the illustrations.

Child-directed shared reading

The child is directing this experience rather than the adult. Your child's reading level and the difficulty of the text will affect what takes place in the session. For example, a child who is not yet reading by themselves might tell the story to you in their own words, using the illustrations and known text patterns. An older child may simply want to read aloud to you.

Joint reading

This is a great shared-reading experience and involves you and your child taking turns reading or interpreting the story.

Repeated reading

The thought behind this strategy is that if children read a text over and over, they will reach a point where they can read it without stumbling and making mistakes. It allows children to become familiar with the words, and therefore process them at faster speeds each time. As they gain speed and proficiency, they gain confidence and reading fluency. Try this technique with your child with a book they love:

* Select the text to be read (depending on age, this might be just one line or a few sentences) and discuss any tricky words with your child.
* Invite your child to read the passage to you.
* Have them retell the passage or story in their own words.
* Invite them to reread the passage again until they manage to do it free of errors and stumbles.

Echo reading

This technique is similar to repeated reading in that there are repeated read-throughs of a text. The difference is that you model reading the sentence or passage first, then your child reads the same text back to you in echo-fashion. This technique not only helps with fluency, expression and reading difficult words, it will also help your child learn an appropriate reading rate. This is important, because reading too slow or too fast can disrupt their comprehension of what's being read.

* Read aloud the selected passage, modelling pace and expression, paying attention to the punctuation marks as you go.
* Have your child read the same sentence back to you using the same pace and expression.
* When your child has gained confidence, swap roles and you be the echo reader, following your child's lead!

Dialogic reading

This reading technique is worth its weight in gold! It can be used with the youngest of children right through to older accomplished readers.

I like to use it in conjunction with other reading experiences, and it's the one that is guaranteed (and backed by research) to increase a child's reading skills.

Dialogic reading is all about questions and how these questions drive a conversation about what's being read. The questions might be about incidents in the text, story components, new words or ways to relate the text to your child's world. This technique also allows you to model how good readers think and make sense of the text they are reading.

There are two acronyms to help you remember the types of questions to ask: CROWD and PEER. You don't have to ask every type of question and you don't have to ask them in order. You can download a bookmark template from my website. Using this CROWD PEER bookmark will help you generate questions as you read with your child.

C a completion question

R a recall question

O an open-ended question

W a who, what, when, where or why question

D a distancing question

P a prompt to encourage the child to make a comment about the story

E evaluate your child's response

E expand on your child's response

R repeat the prompt and praise the response

To illustrate this technique, I've used the first chapter of *Dino Hunter*, the first book in D-Bot Squad – a chapter-book series I co-wrote under the pen name of Mac Park for children from five to eight years old.

Sample reading session

Let's see how it's possible to weave this technique into a child-directed shared reading experience. If they're an early reader new to chapter books, you may want to pause and talk to your child after each double-page spread. If they're managing well, you may choose to talk only at the end of a chapter.

We'll use PEER at the beginning of the book, CROWD at the end of the first chapter, and child-directed shared reading with reading strategies throughout the chapter. We'll also use PEER as a recap strategy at the end of the first chapter to set up the next reading session.

Point to the titles and read them aloud. **Dino** and **hunter** are two words your child is likely to meet a lot when they begin to read, and this is a good opportunity to introduce them.

ℙrompt

Adult: I bet you can guess what this book might be about.

Child: Yeah, it's going to be about a boy who flies dinosaurs.

Evaluate

Adult: I think you might be right, but take a closer look at what he's flying.

Child: It's not a real dinosaur. It's a robot!

Expand

Adult: Hmm. A boy flying a robotic dinosaur in a book called *D-Bot Squad Dino Hunter.*

Child: I think D-Bot Squad might be a special club.

Repeat

Adult: Ooh! Interesting. So what do you think this book might be about?

Child: I think it might be about a boy who joins a secret club that hunts dinosaurs using robots that look like dinos!

Adult: I think you might be right. Let's read the back cover and see.

Ask your child to read the back-cover blurb and confirm or revise their thinking. They may have trouble with the words **everything, anything** and **normal.** If your child can't read these words straight away, tell them what they are. They will meet them again in the book and can practise reading them. Now head to the title page and read who the author and illustrator are before turning to the first chapter.

Chapter One

Hunter Marks ran into class.
He was happy! Book Week was
here at last.

Hunter loved books. He loved
books about dinosaurs the most.
He loved anything about
dinosaurs!

You child might read **everything** instead of **anything** in the last sentence of the first page. In this initial read, both make sense in the sentence so let it go. The interruption will only cause a break in comprehension.

Hunter sat at his desk and
looked around the room.
Everyone was dressed up for
the Book Week parade. *There
are lots of super heroes*, Hunter
thought. He looked down at
his dinosaur book on his desk.
But I'm a dinosaur hunter!

The harder words on this second page are **around**, **parade** and **heroes**. If your child stumbles on the word **around**, encourage them to read on to the end of the sentence and ask them what word they think would work here. If your child has experience of dressing up for a Book Week parade, they will be able to guess the word **parade** by drawing on their prior knowledge. Ask them what they usually do when they dress up as a character for Book

Week to prompt them if they need help. They will have an opportunity to read this word again on page 6 for consolidation! Likewise, their prior knowledge will help them read the words **super heroes**.

Just then, two boys dressed as super heroes came and stood at Hunter's desk.

'What are you?' Super Boy asked.

'You're not dressed up at all,' said Bat Kid. 'You're nothing.'

'I am so!' Hunter said. He tapped the book on his desk.

'I'm the dinosaur hunter from this book,' Hunter said. 'I know all about every dino in here. So there!'

'You and your dumb dino thing,' Bat Kid said.

'We're sick of it!' Super Boy added, pushing Hunter's dino-model over.

Notice that I have repeated the use of the words **super heroes** on page 4 for consolidation. Your child should manage this double-page spread well. They will know **dino** in 'dino-model' but perhaps struggle with the word **model**. Tell them this word if they do. They'll have a chance to meet it again and read it on the next double-page spread.

You might offer to read this spread yourself if your child prefers. This technique can work wonders at about the halfway point in a chapter – children always love to be read to, and a little break like this allows them to sit back and enjoy the story. Encourage them to follow the words as you read so that they get the maximum benefit of having you as a reading role model.

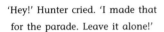

'Hey!' Hunter cried. 'I made that for the parade. Leave it alone!'

Bat Kid and Super Boy laughed and walked away. Hunter stared after them and kicked the leg of his desk.

Crash!

*And leave **me** alone, too,* he thought.

Hunter picked up his dino-model. He put its head back in place. Then he turned the dino-model around to face him. *How could anyone get sick of dinosaurs?* he thought. *Ahmed and Tom are so weird!*

6

7

The harder words on pages 8 and 9 are **window, mind** and **amazing**.

If your child stumbles on the word **window**, direct them to look for clues in the illustration and ask what they think would make sense here. This is a tricky word, and you'll notice that I have repeated it three times on this spread. It will give your child a chance to guess it, read it again and then read it a third time smoothly and with confidence.

Tell them the word **mind**.

If they can't read the word **amazing**, encourage them to skip it and read on to the very end of the page. Now ask them to suggest words that would work in this sentence. They might suggest **incredible, crazy, unbelievable**. Say these are all excellent suggestions that could fit, and ask them what they think about the word 'amazing', if it wasn't suggested. Ask if they think that word could work.

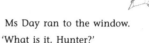

Ms Day ran to the window.
'What is it, Hunter?'

'A real dinosaur!' Hunter said, hopping from foot to foot.
'It flew over the Year 5 and 6 block. Didn't you see it?'

Hunter looked out the window. His mind was busy making lists. Lists of dinosaurs. And lists of dinosaur facts.

Ms Day clapped her hands. But as everyone else sat down, Hunter saw something amazing. He jumped from his seat. 'Miss, miss!' he cried. 'Look, out the window! Hurry!'

Pterodactyl is a very challenging word. You'll notice I've provided a phonetic spelling of the word in the illustration. Encourage your child to read this version. That said, I find that kids who like dinosaurs know all the correct names for many of them, so your child may have no trouble reading this word at all!

'Oh, Hunter!' said Ms Day kindly. 'What a story! You can write about it for me in your writing book.'

Everyone laughed and Hunter's face felt hot. 'I really did see it. It's not a story.' Hunter opened his dino-book and pointed to the page.

'It was this one!' he said. 'It was a pterodactyl, and there was something in its beak. The pointy thing on its head is called a crest.'

Pterodactyl
(ter-a-dak-tal)

Legs

Crest

Wings

Teeth

10

11

Sit back and enjoy your child reading the closing pages of this chapter. They have done well.

'Stop telling lies,' Bat Kid yelled.

'There are no such things as dinosaurs any more,' Super Boy said. 'And everyone knows it.'

Hunter stamped his foot. **Stomp.** He hit the window with his hands. 'It was out there. I saw it. **It was real.**'

'Everyone sit down now,' Ms Day said firmly. 'Hunter, can you take these books back to the library for me? The walk will do you good. No dinosaur hunting along the way. Okay?'

When they've finished reading, use CROWD to end the reading session.

Completion question

Adult: Hunter Marks went to the book parade as a _____.

Child: Dinosaur hunter!

Recall question

Adult: Do you remember what Ahmed and Tom did?

Child: They were sick of Hunter going on about his dinosaurs and they broke his dino-model.

Open-ended question

Adult: Why do you think the boys made fun of his book parade dress-up?

Child: I think they thought it wasn't very good. Like, boring.

W Five Ws question (i.e., who, what, why, when, where)

Adult: What did Hunter see out the window?

Child: A real pterodactyl!

Distancing question

Adult: How do you think Hunter felt when no one believed him?

Child: I think he was embarrassed and a bit angry and upset.

You could also use PEER here to further discussion.

Prompt

Adult: What do you think is going to happen next?

Child: Well, I think he really did see a dinosaur. So maybe . . . I don't know.

Evaluate

Adult: Yes, it was a pterodactyl. That's a bit cool!

Child: I know!

Expand

Adult: Pterodactyls are enormous, dangerous even, and in a school playground . . . YIKES!

Child: Yep, they have such big wings, but I think Hunter is going to try and catch it.

Repeat the prompt

Adult: Well, I can't wait to hear what happens in the next chapter. What do you think will happen?

Child: He has to catch it. But what about the secret club? He needs to join the secret club first: D-Bot Squad! Maybe on his way to the library something happens.

What if you don't feel comfortable reading aloud?

There are a number of reasons why some adults would prefer not to read aloud. If you fall into this category, here are some great alternatives so that your child doesn't miss out. Although they're electronic, they replicate the read-aloud process exactly as though you'd do it, with no distracting electronic game or interactive features – just you, cuddling your child and enjoying top-quality stories read by others, including a few famous people!

Audiobooks

As your child moves past the picture book stage, use audiobooks from sites like Audible and have them follow on with the hard-copy book.

Start small at first. Listening is a different skill, and it's a good idea to build up session length. Be sure to choose books that match your child's interest and age level. We'll look at this further in the chapter called 'Finding just-right books for any age'.

Text-to-speech software

You could also use some text-to-speech software for other reading material. Search for Natural Reader – this software can turn almost any file, including ebooks and even printed material, into spoken word and offers a host of languages, voices and accents, and you can pick your speed. There are quite a few text-to-speech software programs out there, but I think this one is brilliant.

Natural Reader is a godsend for an older child with dyslexia who has research and reading to do and is really struggling to cope. The software highlights what's being read aloud, so they can look at the words as they hear them, which will also help with their literacy learning. This software will save a struggling older reader, and no, it's not cheating! It's exactly the support they need for their learning.

Story Box Library

This site, storyboxlibrary.com.au, is the most invaluable site on the internet. Truly!

It's a subscription-based, educationally sound website created for children to view and hear quality picture books read by local authors, illustrators, actors and storytellers. Your child can have the experience of being read aloud to by all kinds of people, and it's a feast for the eyes as well. You can use it at bedtime, as a read-aloud model, or for a shared-reading experience. The choice is yours!

For just $4.99 (at the time of writing), you can have access to a world of carefully curated books per month. Story Box also does gift vouchers – at $39.99 per year, what better gift than the gift of literacy? You could ask extended family to chip in for a subscription as your child's birthday present.

Hop onto the site now and use the free preview with your child. You'll love it, I promise! If you pick titles to share with your child in advance, try to get a copy of the same book from your local library so that your child can enjoy holding a physical copy as you watch the video again and again. They will love to explore their own book after the viewing as well.

YouTube channels

There are loads of great YouTube channels that read children's books aloud. They may not be at the standard of the Story Box Library, and you'll have to put up with the ads, but you'll be able to find plenty to listen to with your child at these channels:

* Read To My Child
* Nana Kate's Corner
* StoryTimeWithMsBecky
* Storyline Online
* Children's Books
* Storytime with Ryan and Craig
* Books Read Aloud for Children

Enlist the reading powers of others!

Anyone in your child's life can make an impact with books. Share some of the reading techniques in this chapter with extended family and friends, even the babysitter, and encourage them to read aloud to your child.

* Pack books in your child's backpack when they go on playdates or to family to be minded.
* Go to story time at your local library as regularly as you can.
* Keep an eye out for special author readings at local bookstores and other venues.

And remember, children are read aloud to at daycare, preschool and school.

To view my top read-alouds for toddlers, as well as my top picture books, early chapter books, and books for tweens and teens, head over to the 7 Steps section of my website.

Takeaways from this chapter

* It's never too early to start sharing books with your child.

* Reading aloud to a child in the early years is the single most important thing that you can do to help them on their literacy journey.

* Remember, it's not just their brains that gain from reading aloud; their hearts do too.

* Encourage young children to 'read' familiar stories in their own words.

* In the early years, if your child uses an incorrect word when they're reading but it makes perfect sense in the sentence, let it go.

* Minimise the use of electronic formats with bells and whistles. Games and extra features distract from the reading experience and are found to be much less effective than hard-copy books.

* Make use of the various reading techniques to vary your shared-reading sessions.

* Perfect the dialogic reading technique and use it in the early years as well as right through primary school.

* Keep reading aloud to your child for as long as you can.

* Use the alternatives for exposing your child to shared reading if it really isn't your thing, or if you're too tired and time poor.

* Ask for a subscription to Story Box Library as a gift for your child.

'If you want your children
to be intelligent,
read them fairy tales.
If you want them
to be more intelligent
read them
more fairy tales.'

– ALBERT EINSTEIN

Step 3:
Linking writing and reading

Will is sitting at the kitchen bench tracing letters on an iPad screen. He laughs and cheers as the screen fills with a burst of colourful balloons and stars on completion of his last letter.

He is just four years old, and his mother tells me how difficult she finds it to get him to do anything with pencil and paper. She gestures to the crowded corner of the kitchen bench where containers of pencils, markers and crayons fight for space along with craft paper, notebooks, scissors and glue. Instinctively, she knows that tracing on a screen is just not the same and that something important, some special ingredient, will be left out if he has a diet of only this. She tells me how much he rails against any form of traditional writing and drawing, and how difficult it is to break this pattern.

I ask her if he likes to paint and she nods. Does he like using outdoor chalk? Using markers on a whiteboard that is a just-right-for-Will size? Writing secret messages and hiding them around the home? Her smile grows wide, and I know that something I've said has hit the mark. She tells me how she remembers making invisible ink when she was young using baking powder and lemon juice, and how much she enjoyed creating secret messages.

Within seconds she's made her secret concoctions and is demonstrating how invisible ink works, and she's right. Will is hooked from the get-go, the iPad pushed to the side. In no time, he's writing secret letters with lemon-juice solution for his mum to discover. She smiles and says, it's a paintbrush, but still . . . I tell her a paintbrush is bang-on, and suggest that she repurpose old markers for invisible-ink pens too – whatever it takes. I add that it doesn't take much: just fifteen minutes a day.

⌾ FACT

Experts say that just fifteen minutes of handwriting each day is all it takes for children to receive the benefits from writing by hand and its critical role in learning to read.[1]

Invisible ink recipe

Bicarb soda and acid from limes, lemons or grapefruit react with each other, producing changes on paper.

What you need:

* two small containers
* paper
* paintbrushes and/or cotton buds
* bicarbonate of soda (normal household baking soda)
* water
* juice of a lemon, lime or grapefruit
* food colouring

Instructions

* For the invisible ink solution, mix ¼ cup bicarb soda and ¼ cup water together in one of the small containers.
* For the reveal solution, mix juice of a lemon or lime with a little food colouring in the other container.
* Dip a cotton bud or paintbrush into the invisible ink solution and paint a secret message on some paper.
* Allow the secret message to dry.
* Paint over the invisible ink with the reveal solution and watch as the secret message is revealed.

Can writing by hand really make a reader ?

Absolutely. In fact, a child may well be hard-pressed to crack the reading code without it. In turn, reading really can make a writer, too.

In the 1980s and '90s, there was a massive movement to get the message out about sharing books and reading to and with children from birth. Now we all know about the benefits and the impact this has on literacy learning for children at school. And we all know that the more children read, the better readers they become. We share books with children in the early years, and we know why we must – it's no secret anymore. It's the other half of the reading secret that needs to be championed now – writing by hand.

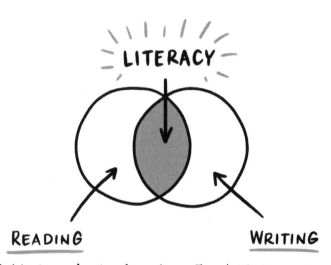

LITERACY

READING

The ability to understand words - decode and comprehend them

WRITING

The ability to produce those sounds - spell them and compose with them

What's changed for our Gen Alphas?

Reading and writing really are like breathing in and out – literacy acquisition doesn't occur readily or at acceptable rates when one or the other is removed or significantly reduced. Enter the technology boom and its impact on Generation Alpha.

Our early Gen Alphas have been the guinea pigs in an unplanned experiment involving screens. Think about this:

* They are the first and the only generation to interact with these technologies from the cradle.
* As a result, they are the first to write less and tap and pinch more.
* They spend more time on technology in their early years than any group preceding them.
* Because of this, they are also the first group studied and researched to assess the impact this is having on learning.

⚡FACT

As children write and make letters, as they write and join those letters to make words, as they write and join those words to make sentences, they are creating something that they can read, because they wrote it. It's their thoughts, their words, their spellings, their learnings – and all the while, they're laying it down in their muscle memory and committing it to their long-term memory.

What's the outcome?

The message from the research is clear: children who begin school with limited writing experience and too much reliance on screens are the group most at risk of falling behind in learning to read and performing at standard year level. Writing is needed more than ever to compensate for technology. We now know that tapping, swiping and pinching cannot displace gripping, scribing and writing.

Don't get me wrong. I'm not saying that technology is destroying Gen A or that it should be taboo. Technology is a vital tool and a skill set that these kids will need. Today, technology is incorporated into the curriculum and has a strong and necessary presence in the classroom. It provides new and important ways of learning, and will be fundamental in their adult working lives way more than it is, currently, in ours.

But that doesn't mean that the old ways must go. It's not about one or the other, but rather about making sure young children write by hand as much, if not more, than keyboarding. We know that children in the preschool years are writing by hand less than ever before,[2] and that's the biggest worry. We need to tame children's tech habits so that they use screens in a balanced way and have the opportunity to reap the rewards from handwriting.

What's the research saying?

Teachers have always intrinsically known the importance of writing by hand. Now science and studies of the brain have finally caught up with them, and the findings are conclusive: we need to fight the good fight on the handwriting front.

Numerous studies have confirmed that writing by hand strengthens the learning process, whereas typing only on keyboards can damage it. High-density brain-scan studies have proven that different parts of the brain are activated when we write by hand versus the parts activated when we type or keyboard. And when we write by hand, those parts of the brain remain activated long after we've stopped writing.[3]

Most importantly, but not exclusively, the parts that remain activated are in the areas for language, for thinking and for laying down of memory – the working memory, where we store and manage information. Keyboarding simply cannot replicate this.

Evidence also suggests that drawing each letter by hand improves letter recognition. A study showed that children aged three to five were better at recognising letters when they learnt to write the letters by hand as opposed to typing them on the keyboard.[4]

But how does this work? And why doesn't it happen with typing? Well, according to the scientists, it's all in the hand and finger movements.

This is what happens in young children's brains as they move pen across paper to form letters:

1. When children write by hand, the movements required to do so leave a motor memory in the sensorimotor area of their brain – the areas of the cerebral cortex responsible for memory, learning, speech and other higher mental and emotional processes.
2. This stored motor memory helps children retain and recognise letters.
3. They then call on the sensorimotor memory for visual recognition of letters and words when they learn to read.

This is what happens when young children arrive at school not having had enough opportunity to move pen across paper to form letters:

* They won't have laid down those strong letter motor memories, and, therefore, won't have them to draw on when they begin the process of learning to read – in short, their ability to retrieve letters from their memory will be impaired.

* They may have poor letter recognition.
* They may struggle to reproduce letters on paper.
* Their fine motor skills (use of smaller muscles in the hands needed for using pencils, scissors and other tasks) may be underdeveloped.
* They will find it harder to learn to spell.

When adults step into kids' shoes

As adults, we've been reading and writing for so long we've forgotten what it's like to learn these skills, or what the skills and the hurdles and stumbling blocks even are! This is what transpired when scientists put adults to the test of writing by hand, keyboarding and learning to read as though they were young children again.

Two groups of adults were assigned the task of learning to write an unknown alphabet of about 20 letters. The first group was taught to write these letters by hand. The other used keyboards.

At the three- and six-week mark, each group was tested for letter recollection, speed of letter recognition and the ability to distinguish correctly written letters from reversed letters. The group that learnt writing by hand came out best in every test, with MRI brain scans showing activation in key areas of the brain. The group who learnt using keyboards underperformed consistently and showed little or no activation in these brain areas.

So, Will's mother was right to worry that a diet of keyboarding and screens wasn't going to cut it. She was right to think that Will was missing out on something special and critical for learning every time he refused to pick up a marker or pencil. That Gen Alphas are writing far less in these years than any other generation does need addressing.

These little hands are still developing, however, and we need to ensure we don't rush them along too soon with handwriting and cause a train wreck. It's important to be aware of their muscle development when it comes to pencil-holding and gripping.

Does pencil grip really matter?

You bet it does! A child's pencil grasp will make all the difference when it comes to writing effortlessly, efficiently and for longer lengths of time. Helping them to master the preferred dynamic tripod grip will set them up beautifully for typing and keyboarding later. However, they won't typically be ready to master this grip until they are between five and seven years of age, as pencil grip requires strength and control of the smaller muscles in the hand.

It's good to be aware of the type of grip appropriate for a child's age and to encourage that grip, but don't worry if your child is a little slower to reach these milestone grips. The stages are just a guide, and most children will get there in their own time. If they continue to miss stages and not progress, you might want to ask the advice of an occupational therapist who can recommend activities that will help develop your child's fine motor skills.

Likewise, it's just as important not to rush a child towards a tripod grip. A three-year-old's muscles won't be developed enough for a tripod grip, and pushing it may only produce incorrect habits that will be difficult to undo.

1 PALMAR SUPINATE

12 – 18 months

This is a fisted grab with the thumb wrapped around the top.

2 DIGITAL PRONATE

2–3 years

All fingers hold the pencil but the wrist is turned and the palm faces downwards.

3 STATIC TRIPOD

3–4 years

Usually three, but sometimes four fingers and thumb grasp the pencil, with most finger pads resting on it.

Often the fourth and fifth fingers do not tuck into the palm.

Usually around the four-year-old mark, children will begin holding a pencil in a three-finger grasp, although sometimes a fourth finger might be used. As they get better at holding the pencil, the ring and little fingers begin to curl into the palm, and children move into a proper dynamic tripod grip that looks like this.

 ## DYNAMIC TRIPOD

4-7 years

The first two fingers hold the pencil that rests on the middle finger.

The fourth and fifth fingers are tucked into the palm and the pencil held at an angle.

As a broad guide, children tend to master this grip sometime between five and seven.

Getting their hands on the good stuff!

Using the right pencils, markers and pens for the stages of development will support children in naturally developing a dynamic tripod grip by the age of seven. Look for pencils and pencil grips that support the dynamic tripod grip. These will encourage your child to write with the correct grip and ensure the whole process is more comfortable and efficient.

And then they go to school

Once children are at school, writing, just like reading, is one of the most important skills they need to master, because they use it and need it in every subject area. Writing also gives children a voice to share their thoughts, ideas and creativity. But it is not a quick process and it is most definitely a journey – an ongoing one that we should make as enjoyable as possible.

I say I'm a writer. I work at writing for a full-time job, so I must be, right? Well, I can promise you this: I am still learning my craft, and I hope to keep learning and improving until the day I put my pen down for good. It's still a process for me, even at this stage in my life. So, what exactly goes on with writing once they're at school?

Really random fact

The first ever writing was to make a list. You know what I'm talking about, don't you? That thing we all do now in the notes app on our mobiles?

Preschool and the first year of school

During these years, children will learn to form letters correctly. Remember, handwriting actually trains the brain, and the writing of letters lays down memories that they will draw on in order to write fluently later. So, let's make those memories accurate ones by ensuring children write letters with the correct starting points and directions, until it becomes automatic and accurate.

This is the key to success because correct letter formation leads to fluent, fast writing later, and that's what every child needs. It is easier to learn a good habit from the get-go rather than changing a bad habit learnt too early.

At this stage, children will also learn about the sounds letters represent, and begin using that knowledge to write and spell words. Eventually, they'll be able to write simple sentences that they and others can read.

Know that their writing will contain lots of approximating (guessing at how written words and sentences should be) and that it's important to value this as part of the learning process. Encourage and delight in it. Be your child's writing cheer squad!

Teachers will analyse their approximations to inform how to guide them best and move their writing forward, so don't stress too much that their spelling and phrasing isn't bang-on. They're learning by experimenting, and we don't want to crush that!

Years 1 and 2

These are the years that a child's writing tends to really take off. They begin to put a number of sentences together and start to write lovely little stories. In class, they will be asked to examine their writing to see if it makes sense and if there's anything they want to fix or correct. This is the beginning of self-editing their work, which will continue and build right through school.

They'll be book-making, journalling, storytelling, contributing to class books and texts, and starting to learn about the different reasons we write: to inform, to entertain, to instruct and so on. At the end of Year 2, children will be planning what they will write, and reviewing their planning to see where they might improve things.

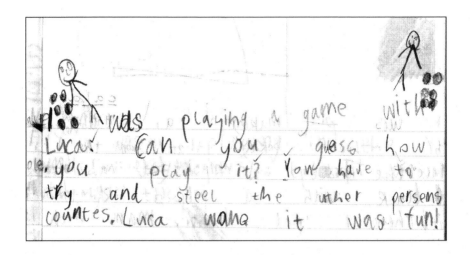

This is also the time when learning difficulties usually become obvious and need to be addressed. Children who are struggling with reading and writing in these years will need extra support to ensure they avoid falling further and further behind. It's the reason the class sizes in the first two years of school are kept smaller. Evidence shows that a child going into the second half of their primary school years with difficulties left unaddressed rarely closes the learning gap with their peers; in most cases, the gap gets larger.

The later primary years

From Year 3 onwards, children are really expanding their repertoire of writing skills. They will know that writers work on and craft their writing; that a quality piece of writing needs to be edited, improved and honed to a final piece. They will focus on story structure and the elements of good story writing: setting, tension, plot, character and more. They will organise their arguments and ideas in paragraphs, and consolidate their knowledge of nonfiction texts. They will employ all their skills of grammar, sentence structure and spelling to draft and redraft what they've written with a clear sense of their audience in mind. They will lay out their writing using features including headings, bullet points, labelled diagrams and borders, and present their writing using presentation software and desktop publishing. And they will refine their note-taking skills in readiness for high school.

In these years, technology will be ever-present and incorporated across all their subject areas. It's tempting to let writing by hand slide, but much will be lost if we do. These are the years when children are consolidating their writing skills, mastering their spelling, sentence structure and grammar, learning how best to structure texts for maximum oomph! And as they do, they commit it all to memory – strong brain memories that will be drawn on right through high school and for the rest of their lives.

When children write by hand, they are in the driver's seat. They form their thoughts and they jot them down. They draft their piece, read it to see if it makes sense, correct, self-edit, review, and panel-beat the whole thing into shape, all the while bringing their knowledge of all these things to the fore and thus further consolidating their skills.

On computers, by contrast, they relinquish that drivers-seat role. Autocorrect, predictive text, spellcheck and grammar checker all kick in, and those crucial areas of the brain check out: no more laying down memory and committing it to the long-term, no more calling on memory to revise and consolidate learning, because the computer automatically does it all for them, and in such subtle ways that most of the time they're unaware it's happening. There's no time to consider if a word looks right, if it's been misspelled, if there's missing punctuation, if anything! Why would you? The computer is doing it all for you.

When I run writing workshops in schools, I have a hard and fast rule: no one goes near a computer or device until they are close to a final draft. I prefer to have them complete the final draft by hand as well. I encourage this not just for all the benefits to their reading, writing and spelling, but also for their creativity and writing capacity.

Writing by hand stimulates ideas faster

A writing study conducted by a professor from the University of Washington looked at groups of children in Years 2, 4 and 6. It revealed conclusively that the children in the study who were writing by hand wrote more words, wrote faster and expressed more ideas than those who were keyboarding. MRI imaging confirms that writing by hand activates the creative thinking area of the brain. Again, it's the movement of the fingers in writing by hand that does this.

The perfection-presentation generation

A chapter on writing by hand would not be complete without a note on the value of what I like to call homemade design, layout and illustration.

Remember doing bubble writing at school? Block letters with drop-shading? Fancy borders? Swirly-fancy-fake calligraphy? Picture-frame borders? Three-dimensional borders? Doodle-art borders? I was queen of them all. It was one of my favourite things to do – the decorating, the laying out, the headings, the all-of-it.

I miss it so much in classrooms and in children's work that I brought it back in my own Harriet Clare series – diary-style chapter books where the readers get to read Harriet's secret notebooks, and contribute to them. Every ten or so pages, readers are asked to reflect on what they've read and check their understanding so that they can offer advice to the characters or comment on events in the stories. I also suggest they complete borders and create word art, and I get them to draw. I have them add themselves to illustrations alongside the characters, to add their own flavour to these chapter books. Yep, I broke the wall between reader and book, and for very good reason.

I did this not just because I miss all these lovely homemade elements, but because I know its importance. I know its place alongside pristine PowerPoint presentations and perfect desktop-published documents. The end result is a keepsake of their handwriting, their drawing, their art, their thoughts. If they hang onto these books, they'll be able to share them with their own children when they are parents themselves.

The act of writing, of playing with letter shapes to make word art, the borders, the drawing, the critical thinking, the engaging with characters in books like never before, builds readers and literate kids. And that's what we all want.

So I have another rule when I go to schools to do writing residencies; I have them complete their final drafts by hand as well. They publish their work with me completely by hand – no computer-driven layouts, borders, headings or anything else. Because I think, just this once, while I'm with them I am going to value all that each child can do, knowing that it's making them a better reader and writer.

Here are some snapshots from my Harriet series that children from all over the world have completed and sent in to me at Harriet's Blog of Awesomeness. Receiving these, posting them on the blog and writing back to the children as Harriet has been one of the most love-my-job tasks I've ever created. All those children writing by hand, using critical thinking skills, drawing, doodling and reading for sheer pleasure is my bit for all those Gen A kids out there, and I can't thank them enough for picking up a pen, pencil or marker.

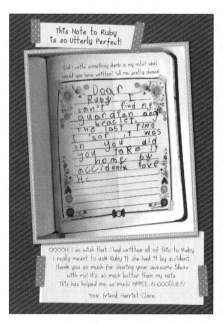

Don't let them stop writing just because you think they can read!

Fifty-eight Year 5 students are scattered about the school's library in groups as they work at the task I've set for them. I'm the visiting children's author doing a writer-in-residence program at this school, and over the last few days I've given general author presentations, run writing workshops, conducted guided writing meditations and done lots of drama and character role-play. I've even donned a polyester T-rex dinosaur costume that stands at 2.2 metres when inflated, and run through the school's main hall, roaring to an audience of squealing, screaming, giggling students. He's a character from my D-Bot Squad series, and the costume is ridiculously popular with the kids.

I won't deny it – for me, working in schools and at readers' and writers' festivals is quite possibly the best part of being a children's author. Interacting with my audience, igniting a passion for reading and writing, hearing what's in their heads, and just observing – it is not work for me.

Today, I'm observing something I see constantly: students who take notes by hand have the advantage over those note-taking on devices. Yes, it's a thing. A scientifically researched and documented thing. As I go from group to group, I register for the thousandth time how little the pen and paper scribers need to refer to their notes when they report back to me, and how the tappers and keyboarders tend to read their notes to me verbatim. Different schools, different students, same same. I see it over and over.

⚡ FACT

Our corticospinal tract is one of the major pathways for carrying movement-related information from the brain to the spinal cord. It is particularly critical for fine finger movements like writing and typing. Science tells us that this tract continues to develop as late as young adulthood. For this reason, handwriting, a fundamental skill that strengthens fine motor processes, must be continued right throughout high school.

What's the deal with note-taking by hand?

If you ask scientists who study the brain, they'll tell you that taking notes by hand requires a different set of cognitive processors to keying notes in to a device or laptop. 'But it takes too long to write notes long-hand and it's so much easier and faster on a laptop. You can get down much, much more. This makes no sense at all!' I hear you cry. And on the surface, I agree with you. Taking notes on a laptop is faster. And sure, we're able to get more down than when we write long-hand. That's got to be a good thing, right?

But the research findings say therein lies the problem. Studies of high school and university students show that those taking notes on laptops, who can type faster than they can write, take more notes than those writing notes by hand – but the typists tend to take down everything word for word, frantically tapping out all that comes from the lecturer, tutor or teacher's mouth. So what's the problem with that, you ask?

Pam Mueller and Daniel Oppenheimer's research[5] is just one of many studies demonstrating that students who write their notes by hand come away with a deeper understanding of the content presented, despite the fact that they wouldn't have gotten everything down verbatim. This is how science says it works:

1. Because writing by hand is slower, students know they don't have a hope of writing down everything verbatim.
2. Instead, their minds aren't on keyboarding every single word and are freer to listen properly and digest.
3. Then the magic happens – to make handwritten notes, the brain has to kick into gear big time and synthesise what's being said. We don't realise it, but to do this we paraphrase and put things into our own words, in order to get the gist down on paper.

4. Because we've paraphrased and summarised what's being said so that we can more succinctly get down the most important information, we retain it and understand it better.

Transcribing notes isn't the same as synthesising what's being said, summarising it in our own words and writing it down in a way that's more meaningful to us. Sometimes we might jot down a sentence word for word; other times we might write down one word and circle it, draw arrows to it or underline something. All these actions help us to store the most important things in our minds – what we've heard and what we've written.

And there are other benefits of writing by hand – as if this isn't enough!

Need any more convincing about this critical puzzle piece in literacy-learning? Here are just some of the many documented benefits from writing by hand for at least fifteen minutes each day:

* promotes an increase in brain activation and cognitive development – thought process, problem solving, language learning, knowledge and skills
* contributes to literacy learning
* improves motor skills
* builds self-confidence – those who write frequently feel more confident in their writing ability
* provides a lift in performance across all academic subjects
* helps with creativity and generating ideas
* provides a solid foundation for higher-order skills, such as critical thinking
* aids with writing fluency – the more readily and quickly you can write, the freer the brain for composing and crafting texts.

For the love of writing

Much has been written and said about teaching to NAPLAN and the need to raise schools' writing scores in response to poor NAPLAN results. These standardised tests that students sit in Years 3, 5, 7 and 9 are used to determine whether or not students are meeting educational benchmarks. Claims that teachers teach to the test only, that they drill the structural features of narratives, persuasive texts, recounts and other types of testable texts to ensure students will know how to structure a piece satisfactorily in a NAPLAN paper, appear regularly online and in other news forms. Claims are rife that teachers are turning students off writing by whittling the process down to sizzling opening sentences to hook the reader, well-structured opening arguments, and other restrictive and limited scaffolds that destroy creativity and lock students into a sausage-factory style of writing instruction. Are these claims accurate?

Evidence-based research shows that there's a definite link between students being engaged with writing and positive literacy outcomes.[6] There's also accumulating evidence that the teaching of writing in classrooms is becoming more and more limited, with less and less room for creativity and self-expression.

However, I know how often I am booked to work with teaching staff and students on lighting a writing spark and lifting the creativity in students' writing. I know how often my colleagues are booked for this sort of work as well. I'm regularly in touch with staff who care about creating engaged and interested writers, who want to tap into student creativity and bring back the joy of writing. What I see is teachers and staff making room for creativity, imagination and self-expression in writing, and nothing could make me happier.

Me doing the NAPLAN test

Not long ago, a publisher asked me to write a book that they could bring out at Christmas, and this meant a seriously mad rush to meet the writing deadline. I had one month to do what would normally have taken me three, and I was just a tad flapped. Time was ticking and I did not have a single idea in my head, knowing that I needed to generate thousands of words in no time if I was to get this done.

I did all my usual no-idea-buster tricks: took a long bath, took another long bath with the addition of red wine and candles, took a shower, swam lengths of the local pool. Is there a water theme happening here, you ask? For some reason, it's always worked for me, but on this occasion my brain refused to play.

Eventually, a very loose plot began to take shape in my mind that I thought had legs. It was enough to send me off to my cupboard where I keep a ready stash of fresh unlined notebooks (I start a new one for every book I write – a little superstition of mine) and I began to scribble, write, draw and write some more. After much scribbling and scratching on paper, I felt I had the bones of a workable story, though it had taken me the best part of a week to get it. I was yet to start the actual writing.

I still have a message I sent to two good writing friends when I was knee-deep in getting this story out. It said: *Who'd be a full-time writer? I am going spare. My bum is spreading, my back is stuffed, my sleeping is non-existent and I am a bad mother, a bad partner, a bad friend, a bad person. I don't remember what outdoors looks like, and no one will know me when I resurface!*

And I'm a writer: a writer who loves her job and wouldn't trade it in for the world. In this particular instance, I was even doing what I called my 'passion' writing – I loved writing that book,

I loved those characters and I loved seeing that story come to life. But to say the journey was pain-free would be a total lie.

Do you know what struck me as I wrote that message to my friends? *This is what we do to our children every time we sit them in front of the NAPLAN writing paper.* We expect children to look at a picture, come up with something amazing to write about it, and bang out a sensational piece of writing – on the spot, with barely any time or luxury to think, percolate, make loads of notes, scribbles and drawings. We expect them to produce a complete and polished text in an outrageously short amount of time, under test conditions. And my next thought was, what kind of horrible thing is that? No baths, no wine, no nothing! I clearly would not cope.

My response to this realisation was to develop an activity to use with as many students as I can get in front of. I've called it my 'guided writing meditation for unleashing creativity'. The activity teaches students to visualise a scene, experience it from a sensory point of view and document details from a visual and creative angle. It encourages students to take themselves out of the testing environment, or any other environment for that matter, and into their creative mind-space for just a few minutes. The exercise allows them to generate ideas, thoughts and information that they can use to craft a piece of writing, even under the gun. Once they come out of the meditation, they make their notes. Then they use these notes to write, and because they know what they're going to write and they have their notes to guide them, there are no blocks!

Afterwards, I always ask how they felt about the writing part and the responses are always the same: they can't believe what they wrote and how easy it was to do it. And I always find what they've written so engaging as a reader – their pieces are so creative and vivid.

Technique and skill, or creativity?

My activity is for unlocking creativity and generating ideas because that's what I think makes a piece of writing sing. Yes, of course, if students know the structural features of the text type they're being asked to write in a NAPLAN test, that's got to be a big help too – I can't argue with that. What I do know is that a diet of scaffolds and skills and nothing more will turn lots of children off writing for life. On the other hand, a diet of creative freedom without teaching any skills is leaving things way too much to chance, and we want everyone to be able to write. There are not too many jobs out there that won't require them to write in one way or another.

I've decided, as I write this book, that its theme is balance. It's come up in just about every chapter and will keep coming up. Children do need balance in the teaching of writing because it requires some knowledge of skill, and ideas and creativity, no matter the type of text they're writing or the audience.

If you were to stand in a school hall and listen as I talk about being a writer and writing with students, here are some of the things you might hear me say:

* If you want to get better at writing, read. If you want to get better at reading, write. Honestly, reading widely is the best thing for writing and visa versa.

* One of the best ways to be inspired to write is to get yourself in front of an author. If you learn one of your favourite authors will be at a local bookshop or participating in an event near you, this is a great opportunity.

* I have learnt from experience that becoming a good writer involves a lot of practice. If you want to be good at soccer, or any other sport, you go to training, you practise, and you play lots.

It's no different with writing. The more you write, the better at writing you will become.

* Like anything, there are skills you need to learn to be a good writer. I wouldn't throw you into the deep end of the swimming pool without first giving you some lessons in swimming technique, and writing is the same. Persevere, learn the skills, then use those skills to make your writing great. Be prepared to work hard for it, just like anything else.

* Write about what you love, what speaks to you, what you want to write about, and the joy will shine in your writing.

* Close your eyes, breathe and tap into your memories. Think about things that you've experienced for good or for bad, think about what you'd love to do and why, where you'd like to go and why. Think of a conversation you had recently that made you feel something, and write it as dialogue.

* If you're stuck for ideas, pick up a pencil and play on paper and ask yourself, 'I wonder what would happen if . . .?'

* Take something you know, something familiar, and do something really strange and unexpected with it.

* My first draft of anything is usually pretty bad. It's just me telling the story to myself. Then I start the redrafts, the edits, the finessing, to make it the best it can be. Then it goes to my editor, who helps me make it even better. Hands up if you've ever done more than ten drafts or edits on a piece of writing? (Mine is always the only hand that's up.) It's nothing for me to revisit my story multiple times as a Word document and then again as designed pages before it becomes a book. That's what writing is.

This list could go on and on, but you can see that I'm an advocate of teaching skill and tapping into creativity. To create engaged writers, we need to take writing to them on their terms, their interests, their passions, and give them the freedom to go for it, to explore, to play, and let's see where that takes them. And this is what can happen when we do.

Before the writing workshop, Harry would always write only a few words and always about soccer.

 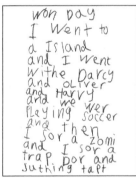 

After the writing workshop, Harry's writing soared. He began writing much longer sentences on a wide range of topics and took to labelling his drawings. He's never looked back.

⌾ FACT

The top ten students of any primary classroom usually have strongly developed writing skills.

Reading like a writer

One of the best ways to learn something new is to look at how it's done by others who are good at it. Share as many quality books with your child as you can. Apart from the enjoyment that this will bring, its impact on learning to read and its role in raising a reader who loves books will also make them better writers. Books teach and show children what good writers do. If they know what good writers do, they can do these things in their own writing. And it will make them better readers as well!

Here are some really simple questions you can weave into your next shared-reading session to focus on reading like a writer:

* Why do you think the author wrote this book? To teach us something? To make us laugh? To tell us a story?
* What did the author do that pulled you into the story?
* What do you think the character is feeling? How did the writer tell you this?
* What were some of the 'magic words' the author used that really caught your attention? Can you find them in the story?
* What things has the author told you about the main character? Can you locate the words that told you this?
* How did the author keep your interest right to the very end? Let's find examples of these things together.

Here is a more advanced example. I'm going to use some pages from my book *Harriet Clare Mystery Dare* to examine how writers show us things about their characters. I use this often in schools, and I do the exercise after we've shared the chapter together – I read it aloud and then we go back and examine the text. They always find everything and then some!

And the **MYSTERY DARE** was this: Finn said there was a secret tunnel going from the kitchen pantry to THE KITCHEN MAID'S CRYING CAVE. I had to take the tunnel to the cave and see if I could find the ghost of the kitchen maid. I stared at him and bit my lip. **YIKES** 😊 ●

Half of me wanted to try and catch a ghost with my **ghost-hunter kit** but the other half was starting to panic.

EClare saved me by saying that we should all go or no one goes. EClare is **THE BEST** brother anyone could **EVER** have!

Then, before I knew it, we were all putting our hands on top of each other's in a GREAT BIG PILE and shouting 'ALL FOR ONE AND ONE FOR ALL!'

Adult: Can you find the sentence on page 70 where Harriet shows us how she is feeling by doing something – an action?

Child: She stares and bites her lip.

Adult: You're right. What do you think she's feeling from this sentence?

Child: She's worried and a bit scared.

Adult: Yes, that's the author telling us how she's feeling by using an action – something the character does.

Adult: EClare says something on page 71 that tells us something about what kind of a brother he is. Do you know what it was that he said and what it tells us about him?

Child: He said that they all had to go or no one goes.

Adult: What do you know about EClare from this?

Child: He sticks up for his sister. He knows she's scared, and he wants to help.

Adult: The author showed us a lot about EClare just from him saying that one thing. It's much more interesting than if the author just wrote: *EClare is a loyal, caring brother!*

Adult: Ooh, we can find out so much about everyone by what they're saying in the speech bubbles.

Child: Yes, like Finn. I think he's a coward. He calls Harriet a chicken and then he says he isn't even going.

Adult: I know! I agree with you. What about Indie? What do we know about her from just those ten little words?

Child: She's a really good friend to Harriet. She's not scared to stand up to Finn for her. I think Finn's a bit of a bully.

Adult: It's amazing how much authors can show us about characters by what they say!

Adult: The author is showing us on page 74 how everyone is feeling by what they're doing – their actions. Can you find them and tell me what you know?

Child: They're all holding their lanterns too tightly. You'd do that when you're scared. They're all freaking out! And they're all breathing a bit funny. I think they're starting to panic!

Adult: I would be too! Wouldn't you?

Child: Maybe. The author uses speech to tell us that Harriet and Freya sure are. Harriet thinks she's going to wet herself! Ha ha! She's really freaking out.

Adult: So, authors show us about their characters by what they do, what they say and what they think.

My last word: nostalgia

Not long after my mother died, I was going through a drawer of items and I came across a letter she'd written. Seeing her handwriting absolutely undid me. I swear I could feel her, hear her and see her in those handwritten words. After the pain of missing her subsided enough to let the beautiful memories come flooding in, I thought to myself: memories really are made of this. And then I smelled the paper. Ha! Sadly, it didn't smell of her favourite perfume, like it would have in a novel, perhaps.

Despite the lack of perfume for a trigger, it struck me that an email or opening a computer file just isn't the same somehow. That's not to say I don't have a pile of saved emails and text messages that I treasure: I do. But what I affectionately call my Box of Life will trump them every time, I suspect. Keep your child's handwriting attempts and make sure they have plenty of your handwriting too!

For my top tips and apps for getting children to write, head over to the 7 Steps section of my website.

Takeaways from this chapter

* Writing and reading go hand in hand for literacy acquisition.
* Just fifteen minutes of handwriting per day is enough to gain the benefits.
* Gen Alphas need to pick up pens and pencils as much, if not more, that they do screens and keyboards.
* The early years are a critical time for writing by hand and laying down motor memories that they will need in order to read and write at school.
* It's important to be aware of the age-appropriate types of pencil grip and to support these stages rather than pushing on ahead.
* Learning to write is an ongoing process, and the more joy we infuse into children's writing activities, the better writers and readers they will become.
* Writing by hand helps with the creative process.
* Value and promote children's handwritten word art, designed headings, layout elements and illustrations alongside computer-generated work.
* Encourage older children to take notes by hand.
* Read and share books with your child as examples of good writing and what good writers do.

'No entertainment
is so cheap as reading,
nor any pleasure
so lasting.'

-MARY WORTLEY MONTAGU

Step 4:

Taming the tech and making it count

- -
....

When I was little, we had a rotary phone in our family home. Later, we installed a push-button phone mounted on the kitchen wall, and I thought it was the coolest thing I'd ever seen! I learnt my childhood phone number by heart, and I can still recite it, even though I haven't dialled it in decades.

Yet I can't recite my children's mobile phone numbers that I call on a regular basis. This is because I've entered my children's numbers into my mobile's speed-dial favourites. I don't need to commit them to memory, and so I don't bother.

It's one small task among many that I've relinquished to technology. And every day, in ways that I'm not even noticing, I allow technology to make my mind lazy. Don't get me wrong: I'm a fan. I'm an all-embracing, tech-savvy, laptop-loving writer, and I'm the first to admit it. But is too much of a good thing affecting my ability to commit facts to memory and recall them easily?

And what's that doing to my brain? At least I can say that at one point in time I did commit facts to memory, but will Gen A be able to say that in their turn, immersed as they are in technology from birth? And what's that doing to their brains?

There is much said about technology and children, and it sparks hot debate around the globe. As more and more research surfaces on technology and screen time in children's early years, serious concerns about its overuse and its impact on learning have taken centre stage, and this isn't changing any time soon. But the findings aren't all bad. Studies also show that active screen time can enhance your child's learning. Confused?

Bottom line – technology is an awesome, valuable tool, and children must learn digital skills. But what is the right age for children to be introduced to it? How should it be used? How much is too much? What are the pros and cons of a childhood immersed in gadgets? Most importantly, what are the signs of technology overuse and how can you make sure your child is not at risk of its negative impacts on learning? Evidence tells us that too much, too soon, *is* detrimental, and usage needs to be closely monitored and limited.[1]

I must confess right now that I think I'd scream if someone tried to take my laptop away from me, and don't even think about touching my phone. Then again, I use notebooks and write a lot by hand – I'm a big advocate of this. But I use technology – a lot. Every. Single. Day. And I would sorely miss it if it was taken away.

I read the news online, research, write, build presentations, chat with groups and friends, shop, stream music and shows, and yes, this hard-copy book lover actually uses a Kindle when she travels – for the sheer ease and convenience of it. Are there as many ebooks on my Kindle as there are books on my shelves in my home? Not even close, and there never will be, but don't anyone dare try to take my Kindle from me either!

All in all, I'm not sure what I would make of someone telling me to pack the screens away now because I've reached my daily limit. So it's heartening to know how much positive research there is showing the benefits of technology.

The good

Technology and future employment

Our first Gen Alphas will enter the workforce around the year 2030. When they do, tech jobs will be in more demand than ever, and almost all jobs will require some sort of computer and tech knowledge. Having grown up with technology will be their trump card.

By 2030, there will be jobs that you and I can't even imagine or get our heads around, and the people filling them will be Gen As. When I finished university, one of my close friends told me that she'd landed a job with a group called Email, and that she'd be working on this thing that would, in the future, help people talk to each other by sending messages through space. I asked her what on earth she was talking about, unable to fathom what her job would entail. At the time, there was no internet or even many fax machines, let alone desktop computers. Anyway, off she went to start a tech career in a field that was then unheard of (and as a woman to boot!), and I began my teaching career. It's a conversation that's never left me, and I sometimes find myself smiling as my inbox fills with emails for me to respond to on a daily basis.

How much difference can a decade make?

Let's look back before we look forward. Here are five technology highlights of the last decade that we might never have imagined in the late 1990s and early 2000s. It's worth noting that there were so many amazing technology breakthroughs that I found it hard to choose only five.

* Do you remember the days before Uber and that amazing Uber app? It seems as though we've had it forever, yet it's only been around for nine years.

* In 2012, Google Maps, followed closely by the Maps app in 2014, revolutionised our driving experience. Most of us said goodbye to the printed street directory once and for all.

* Live online streaming of television and Netflix will quite likely be all Gen A knows. Who'd have thought we'd all be binge-watching the way we do now rather than waiting expectantly for the next weekly episode of our favourite series.

* Augmented and virtual reality exploded onto the market. My first conversations about these new technologies have been very reminiscent of my conversation about email with my university buddy. I need to get my head around these technologies, because the expected growth in these areas is off the scale.

Here are five scientific-based technology predictions for the next decade that are already in train. These were even harder to choose.

* According to *Forbes*, the business magazine that reports on technology, finance, industry and more, by 2020 artificial intelligence (computer systems that can perform tasks that could previously only be done using human intelligence) will create 2.3 million jobs while removing 1.8 million. We can only imagine how much of a game-changer AI will be by 2030![2]

* Gene editing will well and truly establish itself in the next decade, and this technology will allow medical science to eliminate hereditary disease by snipping out those offending bits of genes – just like that!

* Microchip implants won't just be for animals. Humans will have microchips inserted into their hands, and not in case they get lost! These chips will alert the wearer to impending health problems and monitor already-diagnosed conditions such as glucose levels in diabetics.

* Driverless cars and buses will revolutionise our current travel options. Self-driving cars are already real! And by the time our Gen As are old enough to get their licences, driverless cars will be commonplace, so will they even need a licence?

Technology helps develop problem-solving skills

Many video games are centred around 'quest' and 'survival-mode' tropes where the player has to problem-solve their way out of tricky, often time-sensitive situations to progress to the next level. A player needs to brainstorm solutions and trial them under pressure. Thinking outside the box, considering failed attempts and using that knowledge to come up with new strategies are all excellent problem-solving activities.

Technology builds independence, resilience and empowerment

Children are generally the decision-makers when using technology. Whether they are building a presentation in PowerPoint, creating a whole new scene or world in a game, or simply moving and placing a puzzle piece into position, *they* make the choices. They persevere to get through multi-level learning apps and games. They persist when designing and laying out their work until they are happy with their final product. All of this builds independence and resilience.

Technology is great for their imagination

The visual capacities of software and games allow children's imaginations to roam free. What other environment allows them to design, create scenes and see things in 3D, from dressing characters to creating their own avatars and bringing things to life? The sky really is the limit. The opportunity to print your own creations and designs via a 3D printer is set to explode over the next ten years. If they can imagine it, they can create it.

Technology expands horizons and can enhance learning

Technology allows children to see, explore and learn about places and things they might not be able to see in person.

Technology develops spatial awareness, visual attention and reaction times

When children actively participate with actions in quality games and apps – moving things around, adding, outlining and tracing, building – it allows them to explore concepts such as size and shape, it challenges their visual attention span and it develops their spatial awareness.

Technology can enrich language skills

There are many excellent educational apps on the market and interacting with the right ones may help children with their language skills. Apps for vocabulary, reading, interactive ebooks, spelling and even writing can offer a multi-sensory experience that children love.

Technology can open doors!

Could your Gen A child be the next kidpreneur? Technology really does have the power to take children's ideas and turn them into success stories.

* **coderbunnyz.com:** Samaira Mehta is a STEM-savvy ten-year-old who started coding when she was six. Just one year later, Samaira created a STEM interactive coding board game called CoderBunnyz. Since then, she's developed another one to teach the concepts of artificial intelligence and has taken the boardgame world by storm.

* **madebyyuma.com:** Yuma Soerianto is an eleven-year-old Melbourne schoolboy who also started coding at the age of six and who now has seven apps (and counting) for sale. His website for children and adults teaches coding because he believes that anyone can code. His dream is to change the world through technology within the next ten years!

* **Ryan ToysReview:** This eight-year-old boy was YouTube's biggest earner for 2018. Ryan Kaji's YouTube channel began in 2015 and has had more than 30 billion views. The videos show him opening, playing with and reviewing toys with his parents. And he now has a television show too!

The bad

Technology can cause digital dementia

Digital what?! I know what you're thinking: is this woman for real? Well, this is one of the biggest concerns for this generation because it's the one that impacts learning to read most significantly.

'Digital dementia' is a term created by neuroscientist Manfred Spitzer.[3] It's used to describe how an overuse of technology causes a breakdown in our learning, memory and recall – our cognitive abilities. Spitzer's work showcases how our short-term memory pathways deteriorate when they're not used. In short, children wedded to devices are showing signs of short-term memory dysfunction directly linked to their techno-addictions.

FACT

Children's working memories are their reading powerhouse. If their working memory isn't developed enough or they have working memory problems, they will struggle to learn to read.

We've already looked at the effects of too much tapping and swiping and why it shouldn't be allowed to displace handwriting in the earlier chapter on writing. When children write by hand, the movements required to do so leave a motor memory in the sensorimotor area of their brain – the areas of the cerebral cortex responsible for memory, learning, speech and other higher mental and emotional processes. This stored motor memory helps children retain and recognise letters.

'Overuse of devices and gaming consoles hampers the balanced development of the brain.'[4]

– DR BYUN GI-WON, PSYCHIATRIST AT THE BALANCE
BRAIN CENTRE, SEOUL

When they learn to read, they call on their sensorimotor memory again for visual recognition of letters and words. If a child has breakdowns in cognitive abilities, particularly memory and recall from the overuse of technology in the younger years, they will struggle to lay down and store memory. A child who has little exposure to writing by hand and an overexposure to technology cops a double whammy!

As if this isn't worrying enough, overuse of devices can also lead to the development of the left side of the brain over the right. When this happens, the brain suffers an imbalance.

Kids leading device-driven lifestyles are presenting with brain-function issues in numbers never seen before. The damage of this overuse and cognitive off-loading – the handing over or outsourcing of important cognitive tasks to devices, rather than storing information and using their brains – doesn't just impact children's memory-making skills. It also impairs their reasoning skills, attention span, emotional wellbeing and quality of sleep, all of which sets them up for learning difficulties.

Technology can create hand problems

The last thing we want to see is a child starting school unable to hold pencils and operate a pair of scissors. Too much time on devices means less time completing activities that develop finger- and hand-muscle strength. Believe it or not, Gen As are also at risk of early onset arthritis

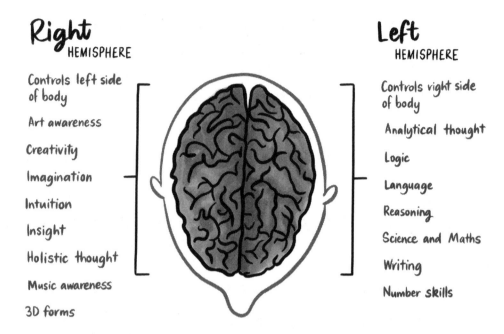

Right
HEMISPHERE

Controls left side
of body

Art awareness

Creativity

Imagination

Intuition

Insight

Holistic thought

Music awareness

3D forms

Left
HEMISPHERE

Controls right side
of body

Analytical thought

Logic

Language

Reasoning

Science and Maths

Writing

Number skills

and carpal tunnel syndrome. Activities such as texting for long periods, overhandling a mouse or repetitive game-console movements all place your child at risk. So common are the thumb and hand problems presenting in medical surgeries and physiotherapy rooms that terms such as 'teen texting tendonitis', 'swiper finger' and 'gamers' arthritis' have entered our vernacular.

Technology can cause eye issues

We tend to think it's just adults working away at computers day in and day out at the office who are most at risk of eye problems, but children's eyes are just as vulnerable, if not more so. Eye issues from too much screen time can be as simple as dry, irritated eyes, or can be more troublesome conditions such as myopia – shortsightedness. And it's true; shortsightedness from sustained periods staring at screens is growing at an alarming rate.

~~~~~~

✧ FACT

When we use screens, we blink less! Normally, we'd blink
about fifteen times a minute. In front of screens, this can
drop to fewer than five blinks per minute.

~~~~~~

As adults, we are more aware of the damaging effects of screens. We know to keep a healthy distance from them, and we can ensure we look away from the screen and into the distance every twenty minutes or so to reduce the negative effects. Children don't do any of these things when they are completely entranced by their electronic game, the television or a device.

Technology encourages multitasking, but that's actually not a good thing!

Olivia sits at the desktop computer in the work area of the living room doing homework. A quick glance confirms that as she's completing said homework online, she also has a number of internet tabs open and is flicking rapidly between them. She's also shuffling through her online music playlists, chatting with online friends, interacting with social media platforms, and pausing once in a while to reply to a text message that's come in on her phone.

Is this a common sight in your home? This is digital multitasking, and while it might sound high-functioning, research says it's anything but, and that we need to teach our kids the importance of mono-tasking.[5] When children are digitally multitasking, their brains are spending enormous amounts of energy responding to information and visuals and making quick decisions. This leaves them with a lot less brain power and fewer resources for actual comprehension and retention.

A multitasking experiment

A class of students was divided into two groups. The first group was allowed to search online during a lecture for related information, as well as check email and undertake other standard online activities. The second group listened only to the lecture. The group mono-tasking – listening to the lecture – outstripped the other group significantly on comprehension, memory and retention of information. This controlled group experiment was completed several times with the same outcomes.[6]

⌀ FACT

Multitasking reduces productivity by up to 40 per cent.[7]

Technology can cause digital distraction and information overload

As a writer surrounded by technology, I learnt this the hard way. Now when I sit to write a novel, once I have a good rough draft on paper and I'm ready to begin a solid first draft on the computer, I do two things: I leave my phone in another room and I open Ommwriter on my computer. This amazing piece of software hijacks your desktop so that you can't see your dashboard – no email, no internet, no social media, no pings, no rings. Instead, what you get is a selection of gorgeous backgrounds, audio tracks and sounds to choose from as you're typing.

In this space, there is you and your writing, and nothing else. It's heaven! In my pre-Ommwriter life, I would hear a ping and abandon my Word document to read the email. Before I knew it, I'd be doing a quick check on social media and wham! Just like that, I'd be sucked down a sidebar rabbit hole – click, click, do I like that dress as much as I think I do; click, click, that hiking trek is just what I'm hankering for. And there would go half an hour of valuable writing time.

If an adult finds it hard to maintain focus, how much harder must it be for a child? These days they're trying to learn in a world full of distractions. There are distractions they like, such as favourite electronic games or texts from besties, and distractions that will find them whether they like them or not, like my sidebar that's curated perfectly to tempt me.

Then there's the bombardment of information that we never had to negotiate as children when we researched something in a book. Online, there is an infinite supply of information, often in small bites and laden with visuals and pop-ups and links to more sites with even more information. In the digital age, information has become cheap, and the constant flicking and leaping from one link to another often means compromised learning, compromised comprehension and compromised attention spans.

Technology can cause speech delays

As the chapter 'Talking their way to literacy' outlines, the critical age for speech development is from infancy to five years. It also examines the importance of oral language for literacy and learning to read.

In these early years, the more a child is absorbed on a device, the less they are interacting, socialising and expanding on their speech. A study found that the more time children between the ages of six months and two years spent using handheld screens such as smartphones, tablets and electronic games, the more likely they were to experience speech delays.[8]

☀ FACT

When children and people are typing on devices, performing tasks on tablets and computers or glued to a show on the TV, our first response always is not to disturb them – they're concentrating, they're busy. It's no different with children, except they really do need us to talk to them and engage with them for the development of social and pre-reading skills.

Technology can disturb sleep

Sleep researchers tell us that sleep is the foundation of all mental and physical health. 'No tech before bed' is a rule that needs to be observed by children and adults alike but especially for children. The use of smartphones, hand-held electronic games and other devices in the hour before bedtime will absolutely affect sleep, whether we realise it or not. This interaction with screens before bed interrupts the production of melatonin – the natural hormone that prepares our bodies for sleep. Brains need dark and silence so that they can get on with the work they need to do as we sleep.

How do you ensure your kid is not at risk of overuse?

If you research what doctors and health professionals are saying, the warning signs for digital dementia make for an extremely distressing list: just a handful of the things you'll find are difficulty in recalling number patterns, directions and names; short-term memory loss or forgetfulness; balance disorders; and developmental delays.

Rather than focus on what could happen, a better and simpler route is to take a proactive approach that will ensure your child is never at risk of developing any of these symptoms. All it takes is a simple review of their digital dependence on a regular basis with a few simple questions. A yes to any of these questions should serve as an alarm bell.

* Does your child like playing and watching videos on devices and television more than playing outside?
* Does your child spend more time keyboarding and pinching, tapping and swiping than they do writing, drawing and creating with pens, pencils, paper and craft materials?
* Does your child have a slouched posture?
* Would your child choose a device over a social activity?
* Does your child get angry when asked to take a break from a screen?

How can you ensure a balance?

The interactive nature of technology entrances kids and offers them so much, and let's face it, it's a handy entertainer for those times when you just need a few minutes. We all use technology to distract, to entertain and to educate, and it is a valuable tool. It can be a godsend on long car trips, and the occasional longer burst on a screen isn't going to destroy a child's brain.

It's when the long periods creep into daily lives by stealth that it becomes an issue. Just like everything else in life, it's all about moderation and balance. How's the balance in your home? Take the quiz to check your family's screen-time health.

* As a family, do you set daily limits on screen time? The total includes devices, computers, televisions at home and at school.

    Yes   No

* Do you have set rules about 'no screen time' situations, such as before bed, before school and at mealtimes?

    Yes   No

* Do you have a rule on no-screen zones in your home, such as in bedrooms?

    Yes   No

* Do you keep a check on how screen time compares with time spent on other activities? Consider, for example, if there's a balance between screen time and writing and drawing by hand? Outdoor activities? Reading?

    Yes   No

* Do you ensure screens are not always the go-to entertainer?

    Yes   No

* Do you strive for a higher ratio of educational rather than entertainment screen activities?

   Yes   **No**

* Do you participate in screen time together?

   Yes   **No**

* Do you model balanced screen-use behaviours in the home?

   Yes   **No**

* Do you keep track of weekly hours spent in front of screens?

   Yes   **No**

* Do you monitor your child's screen-time choices?

   Yes   **No**

If you answered No to more than three questions, it's time to review your family's screen-time policies!

How much is too much?

Australia's Department of Health and the Office of the eSafety Commissioner have guidelines based on extensive research and consultation with health professionals.[9] The daily recommended screen times are inclusive of all devices, laptops and television. These recommendations are designed to help you when setting your own limits as a family.

Brace yourself, this could be a bit scary! It's worth remembering as you read these guidelines that there are some days when you might easily achieve them and others when you know the wheels will totally fall off the cart without the respite screen time can afford. It's all about balance and picking your days! It's also worth remembering that there's no magic amount of time per age group and that it's about the quality of their online experiences and your involvement.

Birth to two

Zero time spent watching television or any other electronic media. It sounds harsh, but it truly is for the best. The findings are conclusive that there is nothing to be gained and much to risk by exposing children at this age to television and gadgets.

Babies and young toddlers need to explore their world, reach milestones and engage with adults and other children to develop their language skills. Use of devices and television in this age band can contribute to speech delay. Watching too much on-screen material at this age will also affect the development of the full range of eye movement.

If you do choose to let them watch a screen, make it count and keep it short. Show your child videos that you've taken of them; watch shows such as *Play School* that are deliberately slow and not chaotic, and that encourage explorative play. Busy cartoons and electronic game apps are absolutely not appropriate for this age group and will only compromise their attention spans and eye development.

Two to five

One hour in total per day is the recommended time that children in this age band should spend watching television and using any other electronic media. They need to be actively playing and learning. The guidelines recommend that where possible, children should not be inactive for longer than an hour at a time unless they are sleeping or unwell.

Children at this age benefit from playing on their own and with other children, being read to, and being engaged in physical gross-motor activities involving things like play equipment in parks, scooters, balls of all sizes and big movement games like Tag, What's the Time Mr Wolf and jumping games that require whole-body movement.

Five to twelve

No more than two hours in total of screen time per day. At this age, they are still developing. They need to be moving, not inactive in front of a screen for long periods. Now is the time to set strict family policies about healthy screen habits so that children grow up knowing the importance of this for their overall health and wellbeing.

Thirteen to seventeen

No more than two hours in total per day for entertainment, electronic media, computers and seated electronic games. While the number of acceptable hours is still somewhat up for debate, it is abundantly clear that three to seven hours per day cannot be having no effect at all. This is a very hard age group to manage, and two hours per day is a tough call; some days will be easier than others. Remember, it all comes down to the quality of their online time, not the quantity.

How can you ensure literacy learning is not compromised by screen time?

The solutions are simple, cheap and easy to do.

* Make sure they read real books. Reading a book rather than a tablet improves memory and will make your child a lover of reading.[10] It also gives their eyes a break from blue-light screens

and will improve reading skills, comprehension and vocabulary. Read aloud to them, read together, and give plenty of opportunities for them to read on their own.

* Get them writing and drawing with pens, pencils and markers as much as possible. Have them do all their planning, thinking, note-taking and drafting on paper. Save computers and devices for typing up final drafts, building presentations and laying out projects. Remember, reading and writing go hand in hand for literacy acquisition.

* Balance your child's use of print media and online sources to give them a break from looking at screens. Hit the public library!

* Encourage as much unstructured playtime in the real world as possible.

* Share the digital experience with young children by doing it together and, more importantly, talk about what you are doing as you do it with them.

* Encourage your child to use their head first rather than immediately asking Siri or Google for answers or automatically going to calculators and web pages.

* Use good old-fashioned puzzles and games to develop problem-solving skills in real-time.

* Play memory games and practise memorising things like shopping lists, phone numbers, passwords and addresses.

* With children, sleep hygiene is important. They need quality sleep, uninterrupted by alerts and text messages. Encourage children to leave their devices in a basket stored in the kitchen or another communal room in the home. Strive for a 'no screens in the evening and before bed' policy. If screens must be used at this time, dim the screen as much as possible.

* Train children to get up and move every fifteen minutes when on computers and devices, including electronic games.
* Turn off the TV if no one is watching it. It can disrupt concentration, particularly in young children.
* Strive for the screen-time allocation to be spent on high-quality apps, programs and games.
* Enforce designated screen-free slots depending on the age and interests of your child: during dinner, before school, while studying, during rest time and before sleep are some of the commonly chosen timeslots.
* Encourage mono-tasking by explaining that your child's brain is like a spotlight that shines best on just one thing at a time.
* Make every effort to avoid the use of screens with the under-twos.

Empower your child for the online world

It's inevitable. Gen Alphas will be living and breathing technology by the time they are ten, and it's important that they develop digital skills for their future. Whether we like it or not, most will have a presence online and across every social-media platform. Data suggests that despite rules about acceptable ages for children to be on various social media, they are engaging online at younger and younger ages.

It's vital that their health and wellbeing are protected by making sure they know how to be as safe as possible in the online world. The World Economic Forum advises that children need digital intelligence (digital IQ), and has identified the following eight key skills that make up a child's DIQ.[11]

* **digital citizen identity:** the ability to build and manage a healthy identity online and offline with integrity

* **screen-time management:** the ability to manage their screen time, multitasking, and engagement in online games and social media with self-control
* **cyberbullying management:** the ability to detect situations of cyberbullying and handle them wisely
* **cybersecurity management:** the ability to protect their data by creating strong passwords and managing cyber attacks
* **privacy management:** the ability to handle with discretion all personal information shared online to protect their own and others' privacy
* **critical thinking:** the ability to distinguish between true and false information, good and harmful content, and trustworthy and questionable contacts online
* **digital footprints:** the ability to understand the nature of digital footprints and their real-life consequences, and to manage them responsibly
* **digital empathy:** the ability to show empathy towards their own and others' needs and feelings online.

For my top digital experiences for pre-schoolers and primary schoolers, and for sites that will help with your child's e-safety, head over to the 7 Steps section of my website.

Takeaways from this chapter

* Technology used in a balanced way can enhance learning and help set a child up for the future.

* An imbalance in the use of technology can have detrimental effects on learning and social and emotional health, including deteriorating memory and memory recall, brain development imbalances, hand, eye and posture problems, sleep disturbances, attention span and comprehension issues, and speech delays.

* Children aged between zero to two years are better off without any screen time at all.

* One hour in total per day is enough exposure to technology and screens for children aged two to five years, while a total limit of two hours per day is recommended for older children.

* Minimise exposure to busy cartoons and games that overstimulate in the zero-to five-year age group.

* Reading real books rather than on-screen books should be encouraged on a daily basis.

* At least equal if not more time should be spent doing handwriting and other activities involving pens, pencils and markers for all age groups.

* Not all digital experiences, games and apps are equal. Make their screen time count by choosing worthwhile, quality experiences.

* Play memory games and practise memorising shopping lists, phone numbers, passwords and addresses.

* Encourage mono-tasking as soon as children start using devices and watching television.

* As your child grows, ensure they have all the eight skills they need for digital IQ.

'There are many
little ways to enlarge
your child's world.
Love of books
is the best of all.'

- JACQUELINE KENNEDY ONASSIS

Step 5:

Harnessing the power of book ownership

It's bedtime, and I'm snuggled up with my four-year-old daughter, who smells of Johnson's Baby Bath and freshly cleaned teeth. Her Mother Goose lamp is on and beside it on her bedside table there is a pile of books. On the shelves beneath is a collection of books: library books, books from my own childhood, books that I have given her or that she's received as gifts.

I select a library book that she has chosen herself and, as I do, I sneakily slide her favourite picture book from the top of the table to the shelf below. The book is *A Proper Little Lady* by Nette Hilton and Cathy Wilcox, and it's been Sarah's favourite for weeks, perhaps even months – I've lost track. I have read that book again and again and again. AND AGAIN.

'Shall we read this one that you chose at the library today?' I ask, fingers crossed behind my back.

'No,' Sarah cries. "'Swish, swish, swish, went the pale blue dress." We always start with that one. I want that one first.'

I smile. Somehow, I knew I wouldn't get away with it – and I know that I won't be getting away with just the one read.

And so we read it again, with Sarah joining in, calling out the lines she knows so well, making all the right sounds for the various items of clothing. We point to the pictures and discuss (for what feels like the thousandth time) what she likes most about the things Annabella Jones is putting on so that she can be a proper little lady. And despite having read it so very many times, I can't help but delight in the joy Sarah derives from it, the way she 'reads' the story by almost reciting it word for word from memory as she points to the lines of text on each page.

After we've finished sharing a couple of other stories, I tell her, as usual, that she can spend a few minutes with some books of her choice before I come back in to turn the light out and say goodnight. And of course, when I return, she's turning the pages of *A Proper Little Lady*.

Some of us might be lucky enough to have owned books we loved as children – the ones we kept on the bedside table and read over and over until the covers fell off. The first serious book crush I can remember was when I was five years old – it was a collection of Hans Christian Andersen fairytales that had full-page coloured plates, given to me when I went into hospital for eye surgery.

Oh, how I loved those illustrations. I couldn't read many of the words, but that didn't matter. I had the tales read to me often and I knew them well. I scoured the pages of that volume for what felt like a year. When I was older, I revisited this book to trace the illustrations using greaseproof paper.

I still have the volume on one of my bookshelves, and it's in good company, sitting alongside stacks of books I bought for my own children when they were growing up. These books will go with them when they set up their own homes and families, and yes, *A Proper Little Lady* will be among them. We all know reading and sharing books is key to raising readers, but do you know the impact actually owning books can have on a child's education?

☀️ FACT

Children who don't have books of their own perform significantly lower in reading tests, are nearly four times more likely to read below their accepted age standard, enjoy reading less, are less likely to read, and are less confident readers.[1]

Book ownership is a very real contributing piece in the literacy-acquisition puzzle. It does matter. And while owning books is no guarantee that children will be lovers of reading, knowing that books are valued and worth possessing goes a long way towards raising strong readers who will go further educationally. It's twofold: children who have their own books, and who are also raised in families with adults who own books, do better in the long run.

A massive two-decade study into book ownership found that on average, across twenty-seven countries, having a library of books in the home propels a child *3.2 years* forward in their education.[2] That's staggering! And the best news is that it doesn't have to be a tonne of them. Experts say that a child who owns just twenty books will reap the benefits.

Book ownership beats all

One twenty-year study[1] conducted the largest and most thorough investigation ever carried out on what influences the level of education a child will attain. Researchers were shocked to learn that books in the home had more effect on children's educational attainment than other more predictable and oft-cited factors like family income, education levels of the parents, the country's gross domestic profit or the parents' occupations.

Some of their findings:

* Regardless of whether families are rich or poor, which country they live in or whether the parents are illiterate or university graduates, parents who have books in the home for themselves and their children increase the level of education their children will obtain.
* Having books in the home is twice as important as a parent's education level.

What's so special about a child's home library?

The thing I didn't tell you about my daughter and her book, *A Proper Little Lady*, was that we'd originally borrowed the book from our local library. We read it together over and over, and when it was time to return it to the library, she'd ask to borrow it again. I knew how much she loved that book, so I bought her a copy of her own.

Boy did we get mileage from it, and so many others like it. For her to be able to revisit that book again and again, whenever she wanted for as long as she wanted, without ever having to give it back, was the best gift I could have given her.

Rereading favourites that children own and have access to all the time does build readers. Here are some of the reasons why.

* Familiarity is wonderful for kids – when children reread books that they own and love, they begin to memorise the text and 'read' the book from memory before they can actually read. Their most treasured and most revisited books are the very ones they may learn to read from! These books will also give them a sense that they are a reader. It's not all that different to children wanting to watch a video over and over again. They learn the story structure and pick up something new with each revisit, except that when they're rereading a favourite book, they're practising important literacy skills.

* Having their own books encourages children to read more and will improve their comprehension and vocabulary.

* Children who own a collection of valued books understand that reading is important.

* Owning their own books gives children pride in ownership. Books should have the same currency as games and toys. That feeling of excitement children get when they share toys and games, or even just from conversations about them with friends, extends to the books they own. Having their own library of books to share, swap and talk about, and adding to their growing collection, is a powerful force for good.

* Children who own books are far more likely to have positive and success-oriented experiences of learning to read and literacy acquisition.
* Children who grow up with books have a greater advantage over those who don't, so it's never too early to start owning them.
* Owning twenty books or more has a proven effect on the level of education a child will attain.

Making sure Gen Alphas don't miss out

The National Literacy Trust's Annual Literacy Survey of children found that one in eleven children in the UK did not own a book of their own, with the statistic rising to one in eight in low-socioeconomic families. More girls than boys owned their own books in an almost 2:1 ratio. Even more worrying is the finding that on average, more than a third of Australian children own fewer than eleven books, especially when we now know that it takes twenty or more to gain the benefits. Generation Alpha is the first cohort ever to have such alarming statistics regarding book ownership.

Today, most children have more game apps, toys and computer games than books in their homes. Children are always going to love toys and computer games. They will also love books if the adults around them show them that they are to be valued and treasured just as much, if not more so. Knowing the direct impact books in homes has on literacy acquisition and how far a child can go in the education stakes can help restore the balance between toy and book ownership.

The adults in children's lives are powerful influencers:

* Parents and other significant adults who ensure that the children in their lives own books in at least equal measure to toys and electronic games and apps are investing in better literacy outcomes for them.

* Parents and other significant adults who value books in the home and are reading role models are helping to raise the level of education their children can attain.

'What kinds of investments should we be making to help these kids get ahead? The results of this study indicate that getting some books into their homes is an inexpensive way that we can help these children succeed. Even a little bit goes a long way. Having as few as twenty books in the home still has a significant impact on propelling a child to a higher level of education, and the more books you add, the greater the benefit. You get a lot of "bang for your book". It's quite a good return-on-investment in a time of scarce resources.'[3]

– MARIAH EVANS, ASSOCIATE PROFESSOR OF
SOCIOLOGY AND RESOURCE ECONOMICS

Growing a child's home library, the cheap way

Growing a child's home library doesn't have to be expensive, even if you do get a lot of bang for your book. Bookshops, discount department stores and online booksellers are always an easy go-to for purchases, and they often have sales. Here are some other alternatives to consider.

* Ask friends and family to give books for birthdays and other days where giving occurs. This simple request will help spread the word about the importance of book ownership as well as helping to build your child's home library. And book-givers will

love knowing that they're helping to make a difference in your child's literacy journey.

* Check out streetlibrary.org.au. This organisation has started a global trend of book-sharing and community-building, and now people are doing their own versions of it. Street libraries are little homes for books that are planted in front yards and other places accessible from the street. In these homes, people place books they think others might like. If there's something there that grabs a child's attention, they're free to take it. Hop onto the site and see if there are any near you. If not, think about starting some up with friends. Swapping books for free is a great way to keep a child's home library fresh and growing at no cost. Not every book a child receives will be one they want to keep forever, but it may hit the sweet spot for another child. Share the love of literacy around and see what comes back.

* If you aren't keen on exploring the concept of street libraries, why not host a book-swapping party? Allow your child to choose books they may have grown out of or didn't click with and bring them to the party. Let them choose the books they want to swap them for.

* Get savvy and buy preloved books from second-hand bookstores and book recycling places such as opportunity and charity shops.

* Hit the garage sales. There's no telling what treasures you'll find in someone else's trash.

* Join toppsta.com and other book-reviewing sites where you can win books to review in giveaways. At Toppsta, advance reading copies from publishers are up for grabs, along with other titles each week. All you have to do is set up a profile on the site and enter a giveaway. If you win a free book, you are expected to write a review of it.

* Scan social media and other sites for bookstore and author competitions and giveaways.

* Book fairs in schools always have bargains at a high discount.

* Magazines are a brilliant way to get even the most reluctant reader engaged. They offer eye-grabbing photos and loads of visual support, activities, short and manageable stories, cartoons and a blend of nonfiction and fiction. Children can dip in and out at their leisure, and there's something for every taste. *National Geographic Kids* and *Double Helix* from CSIRO have science, technology, wildlife, space and our world covered, while *K-Zone*, *Just Kidding*, *Total Girl* and *Poppy For Real* give the lowdown on what's popular in movies, toys, books and life! If you have a Lego fan or a child who likes to build, sign up to the free Lego magazines at lego.com. You'll receive four magazines a year packed with comics, activities and building tips for readers of five to ten years of age. Even if they're not into Lego, they'll love the activities and comics.

* Value author-signed copies of books! If an author is visiting your child's school or local bookstore, chances are your child will want to read their books; owning one that has been signed and personalised just for them by the author makes the ownership so much more special.

Charities that get books into kids' hands

Quality books in children's hands is the single strongest contributor to positive literacy outcomes, but not all Australian children have access to books or are able to own books for various reasons. The impact this has for reading and learning is significant. The facts speak for themselves:

* In the latest Progress in International Reading Literacy Study, Australia ranked twenty-seventh out of forty-eight countries in reading ability. Alarmingly, the research also revealed that approximately one in four Australian students did not meet the minimum acceptable standard of proficiency across both literacy tests.[4]
* Many students from a low socioeconomic background have never owned a new book.
* One in seven Australian children leaves school unable to read and write well.

Several charities work to get books into the hands of some of Australia's most literacy-at-risk children. Here are some. Reach out to them, utilise them, support them.

Dymocks Children's Charities

* Books for Kids Week runs in August, and Dymocks donates one dollar for every book bought in their stores. This money is used to get quality books into kids' hands. So, know that when you buy a book during this week you are helping to spread the book joy!
* The Book Bank program ensures selected students from Years 3–6 get a book of their choice each term, every year. This program reaches more than 2500 lucky students annually.
* Book Bonus helps schools raise funds to buy books that their students want to read.
* Dymocks' crowdfunding initiative helps schools raise money to stock their libraries. The charity works with a coordinator from the school, and they double the value of funds donated to a

school's crowdfunding. School libraries play such an important role in your child's reading journey, and this is a great way to ensure the school offering stays fresh and current. If you think your child's school could benefit from this program, download the expression-of-interest form from the charity's website.

Dolly Parton's Imagination Library, Australia

This is a free book-gifting organisation that aims to inspire a love of reading and raise literacy levels in children everywhere. Once enrolled, a child receives a high-quality and age-appropriate book in the mail, free of charge, from birth to five years of age. The Australian arm began in 2014, and the charity provides all the infrastructure, including managing a secure database, a book-order system, the coordination of book selection and purchasing, and the cost of mailing. You can register your child and check online for availability in your area. You can also register to become a local champion who helps bring the program to cities, towns and communities around the world.

The Aboriginal Literacy Foundation

This charity works to close the literacy and numeracy gap between Indigenous and non-Indigenous children and youth. Among their many programs, which include Digital Literacy Hubs, Literacy and Employment Readiness programs, and programs targeting the specific needs of girls and boys, is the hugely successful Books for Learning program. Knowing that exposure to books in the early years is vital, this program provides books to enhance reading and learning at home. You can help support this charity by making a donation or by offering to fundraise for them.

Books in Homes Australia

Books in Homes Australia's vision is to create an Australia where every child and family has access to books. They provide quality books for children living in remote, disadvantaged and low socio-economic circumstances, and since 2001 they have distributed over 2.5 million new books to children across Australia. Their programs target early childhood, preschool and primary-aged children. There are three levels of preview packs that go out each term:

* **Early childhood program**

  Targeting children aged 0–5 years, this program provides a preview pack of twelve age-appropriate books each term (mostly board and picture books), from which parents can select three books each term for them to keep and read with their child.

* **Preschool program**

  Targeting children aged 3–5 years, this program provides a preview pack of twelve age-appropriate books each term (mostly picture books), from which children can choose three to keep and read.

* **Primary program**

  Targeting children in primary school, this program provides a preview pack of 48 books each term. The books are in four reading levels with a selection of fiction and nonfiction titles, from which students get to choose three to keep and read. This range of books includes picture books and chapter books.

Takeaways from this chapter

* Nothing can replace the power of owning and having books in the home.
* Children who grow up with no or very few books in the home perform significantly lower in reading.
* Children who own no books are nearly four times more likely to read below acceptable standards as they grow.
* Being able to cherish and revisit a book again and again is vital.
* At the very least, books need to have an equal footing with toys and electronic games in the home.
* Children need to see the value and importance of books by owning some and having books in their homes.
* You get a lot of bang for your book, and it's worth exploring ways to own them without having to pay out big money.

'Books are the quietest
and most constant
of friends;
they are the most
accessible and wisest
of counsellors, and
the most patient
of teachers.'

- CHARLES W ELLIOT

Step 6:

Embracing two reading philosophies

The auditorium is filled with primary-school teachers from around Australia. They are attending a conference on writing and, because writing and reading go hand in hand, the program offers sessions about literacy from several interesting angles. In 2018, as part of this program, I was hired to complete an intensive writer residency in a school in South Australia where I worked with students on an individual, small group, whole group and whole class level, and at a whole staff level. I am here because my host teacher and I are presenting our work and its impact as a showcase school, and then I will run some of the writing workshops for delegates.

The keynote speaker is on and owns the stage; she is brilliant, a polished presenter who draws in every one of us so intently that you could hear a pin drop in the room. This keynote is exactly what you hope for at an event of this high calibre, but we are the following act and the whole thing is weak-knee-making. Yet, as I sit attempting to quell my performance anxiety, I know this entire experience is an absolute gift for me. I am just thinking how chuffed I am to be part of it when laughter erupts in the auditorium.

I look up to see a new slide displayed on the giant presentation screens. It's a shot of a double-page spread from what can only be described as one of the worst examples of a phonics reader I have ever seen, and it went something like this: 'Sip, tap, sop. Pat is on top.' And just like that, I am laughing too. It really does read like a couple of lines from a script for a porn movie!

The caption for the slide poses the question: how are our children ever to learn the magic of the written word from such a 'low nutrition' text? And there it is, the first hint at what is known as the reading wars – a debate that has been raging for decades about how best to teach reading. From this one slide I deduce that this group will most likely sit squarely in the whole-language camp and not the phonics and decodable-reader camp.

The next day, my host teacher and I are back in the same front-row seats, listening to yet another excellent presenter. Over the course of the conference, the elephant in the room has been making its presence felt – whole-language approach versus explicit phonics instruction. It's clear to me now that this is a pro–whole-language gathering as far as the presenters go, but I'm not so sure about the delegates.

Then, at question time, someone bravely goes where everyone else wants to but hasn't been game to venture. How does the presenter feel about the strong resurgence of the phonics movement, and the criticism the whole-language approach is attracting?

Before I know it, it's as though I'm in the midst of a protest rally. The presenter is describing the public criticism she herself has received as a whole-language advocate; there is talk of legal advice, social media trolling and orders to take down various things from blogs, websites and social media sites. The auditorium takes on a feverish vibe, with loud cheering and clapping. Energy runs high and some people stand for this presenter, who is clearly fighting the good fight for them about the whole-language approach.

I scan the room and see passion that could rival the crowds at a European soccer match. Well, maybe that's taking things a bit far, but this, I think, is teachers at their best – passionate about their teaching, their pedagogy, their students, and it makes my heart sing, although I have concerns about this seemingly one-sided display.

Then, the presenter declares with force, 'We have never, ever said phonics should not be taught. We have never said that.' And I finally release the breath I didn't realise I was holding.

During the breaks after that feverish rally-type moment, I was asked countless times by teachers what I thought about whole language versus phonics for the teaching of reading and where I stood on the issue of the reading wars. Yes, in education circles it's known as the reading wars – the great divide between the pro-phonics and the pro-whole language reading philosophies – and it's been simmering away for a long, long time. As a parent you may not encounter this until your child goes to school, and if you're lucky, your child will go to a school that uses both philosophies; therefore, you may never encounter it. But as a parent you have the right to know about these two philosophies and why they are both important.

What I know from experience is this:

* For many children, learning to read simply won't happen via the whole-language approach. For some children, no matter how much we encourage them to develop a love of reading, give them experiences with high-nutrition texts treated in context and provide a rich world of beautiful books, the approach will not make them a reader.

* Likewise, a diet of only phonics will indeed destroy a love of reading, do little to enrich and extend vocabulary and may have a negative impact on their comprehension skills. For some children, being able to decode words may hinder their ability to really engage with a text and its meaning.

It cannot be a one-sided thing – one side against the other. It isn't that one literacy teaching method works and the other doesn't. It's both sides working together, along with the other components of reading instruction, that will get everyone over the line. And by that, I mean having everyone able to pick up any age- and content-appropriate text and be able to read it, understand it and engage in a positive way with it.

Children need to be exposed to as many reading techniques as possible so that they develop a suite of skills that they can use. Therefore, they need exposure to both sides of the reading wars. If I could set this in flashing lights, I would!

⚡️FACT

Only about half of the words in the English language can be sounded out accurately using letter–sound correspondence – phonics.

What are the reading wars?

This debate about the best way to teach a child reading has left many educators, parents and caregivers confused, and it has gone on for decades longer than it should. .

If you talk to one side, levelled readers (books graded by reading difficulty that use a natural language approach rather than phonics-based words that are easily sounded out) like the ones most schools send home with their students to be read at night, are out, and decodable readers (books based on words that children sound out in order to read) are in.

The other side will tell you that decodable readers are a 'death by boredom' reading sentence guaranteed to turn children off the joy and love of reading, and will not help grow a necessary vocabulary.

So, is the way we teach most children to read setting them up to fail or sail? What exactly are these two sides of the reading wars, and why is a combination approach better than just one side?

In the red corner: the whole-language approach

The term 'whole-language approach' always makes me laugh because I think it sounds like those not using this approach are only teaching a portion of the English language, rather than the whole!

Whole-language instruction uses interesting and stimulating books with rich, high-quality vocabulary to immerse a child in high-nutrition texts, where spelling, grammar, vocabulary and writing are taught in the context of experiencing the book or text, rather than in isolation. Children taught with this approach are wrapped in a shawl of beautiful books and texts to learn to read with, in a natural way, and while whole language may mean different things to different people, there are some hallmark aspects to this method of learning to read.

* Quality literature and levelled readers are used to learn to read.
* It focuses on the joy and excitement of reading for meaning – understanding what is read is the endgame here rather than accurately reading every single word. There will be plenty of time for that later.
* Children are immersed in a literature-rich environment and encouraged to memorise words, predict or guess words using picture and text clues, read on or start over to work out an unknown word or to consider what would make sense when they meet an unfamiliar word. Sounding out is not the initial recommended reading strategy for an unknown word.
* Reading, writing, speaking and listening combine to create readers. 'Anything I can write, I can read.'[1]
* The focus is on the meaning of texts over the sounds of letters, and phonics is just one small part of literacy learning.
* Children use their prior knowledge of a topic to interpret what they are reading.
* Children use patterns, rhymes and repetitions in texts to help them read.
* Reading and writing for everyday relevant purposes is encouraged.

✳ Children learn to read at their own level, and usually progress through a series of levelled readers where the reading environment is controlled to build vocabulary in a success-oriented way.

While the term 'whole language' might not be as widely used in classrooms today, reading programs and methods of teaching reading based on its philosophies are thriving and are as popular as ever for good reason. If you have school-aged children, you may well recognise some of these terms: guided reading, balanced literacy, top-to-bottom literacy and reading recovery. I'm not going to get into all the different teaching pedagogies out there, and these are just some of the many names you might hear. Whole language can be found in all of these methods and more.

Why is this method important for your Gen A child?

We know that learning to read is about making meaning – understanding what we are reading. This is the crux of it. If we can't make any sense of what we're reading, then we're just decoding and getting nowhere. If it's meaningless, what's the point? So, while knowledge of letter and sound relationships is important, it's just one part of the process. Children need to be able to read for meaning, and the philosophies of whole language have this at its core.

And that's not all! Remember the super skills from the first chapter? Alongside this, when done properly, whole language covers the first, second, fifth, sixth and seventh – that's a big whack of the super skills. (I've given you the list again on the next page to save you flicking back.)

Furthermore, once children are starting to read independently, it is the techniques anchored in whole language that will extend them and make them readers for life.

The super skills

1. **ALPHABETICAL AWARENESS:** the basic understanding that written words are made up of letters of the alphabet and are parts of spoken words

2. **PHONOLOGICAL AWARENESS:** the ability to focus on the sounds of spoken language rather than their meaning – these include things like hearing the rhyme patterns in a list of words, and in the sounds of rhythms that make up words.

3. **ENCODING:** being able to translate speech sounds into the letters that represent those sounds – the sounding out of words to write them

4. **LETTER AND SOUND KNOWLEDGE:** the understanding that the sounds they hear can be represented on paper using letters and blends of letters. The relationship between the sounds and the letters that represent them is fundamental for reading and is known as decoding.

5. **VOCABULARY:** knowledge of the meaning of words and their uses. When children know the meaning of a word, they have a much better chance of being able to read it and make sense of it in a sentence.

6. **FLUENCY:** the ability to read text quickly, accurately and with appropriate expression. This happens when all the other components are so honed that a child does them automatically, freeing them up to access text as a competent reader.

7. **COMPREHENSION:** this is the endgame. When a reader can read, and understand and remember what it is that they've read, they've made it!

The phonics camp will be shouting, 'But they need to be able to decode words using phonics to read!' I don't deny that. They do need phonics as one of the skill sets in their arsenal to learn to read, but a child who is still having to sound out or blend sounds together to read after quite a few years of teaching is not going to advance. By then, they need to be reading with some amount of fluency. A child who is still doing this is going to have trouble making any meaning, because all their energy will be used up making individual words. Phonics is important in the early years, but a child in primary school with only this skill in their reading arsenal is in trouble.

Finally, exposure to quality literature that uses rich and challenging language and offers layers and depths to be explored is fun and much more satisfying! Quality literature also gives them opportunity to problem solve, extend their vocabulary, and relate and empathise with characters and their plight. They escape into incredible worlds they don't want to leave and while they are there, not wanting it to end, they are not just reading but also fostering a love of reading for life.

So rich, quality literature, and the sharing and talking about it, must surely be the backbone of the entire process. But why? Let me ask you this: if you wanted to cook the most show-stopping Peking duck dish for your guests, would you source a quality recipe, possibly from a chef you know is reliably good, or would you use a one-star rated version that you know full well won't taste anywhere near as good? All books are not created equal, and what your child stands to gain from rich, relatable and well-written literature is the five-star Peking duck recipe you want.

I'm not saying phonics-based books are all deserving of a one-star rating. Some are absolutely sensational. They are cleverly crafted to deliver a strong, entertaining and satisfying story. However, I am saying that you need to do your legwork and choose wisely, because many decodable phonics readers are disappointing. (More on this later in the chapter.)

Let their teacher teach them

You are your child's first and most important teacher, but not their only one! One of the most important things a primary-school teacher teaches is literacy. So, try to resist getting caught up in the explicit teaching of literacy to your child unless they're struggling. That's the key job of their primary-school teachers.

Your job is to do the set home reading with them and move straight into the fun lane, where you direct their literacy learning with them in the driver's seat, enjoying the ride and not getting bogged down in a traffic jam of struggle. To do this, read lots and widely with them using the underpinnings of whole language. At school, children should be exposed to a variety of quality literature, but school days are chockers and teachers have up to thirty students, making it hard to reach every child, one-on-one, every day.

The reality is that the one-on-one sharing of quality literature has to come from the child's family, extended family and out-of-school environment. I'm not saying you have to share hours of reading with them every day; any amount of exposure works, and you will be staggered at how much they will learn from pure immersion, and how smoothly their reading journey at school will be as a result. Keep reading with them and to them right through their tweens and into their teens, because this really is the gift that keeps giving.

Sharing wonderful books with your child using whole-language philosophies

I'm going to use a book for younger children to demonstrate shared reading using whole-language underpinnings. In the previous chapter on the power of book ownership, I talked about getting a lot of bang for your book. Jeannette Rowe's lift-the-flap book, *Guess What? Colours* is the perfect example of this, as it can be used with children as young as six months through to children of five or six.

At each of these stages below (taken from the chapter 'Reading their way to literacy'), your child can cut their literacy teeth and learn to read from just one book. They may only revisit it ten times from birth to age five, or they may revisit it many more times. Either way, by the time they are five, they'll have learnt how to read several of the words in their favourite book, if not the whole of the book.

Sharing books between 0–12 months:

* creates a special bond between parents and children
* exposes children to the sounds and words of language
* develops a growing awareness that books are just as important and valuable as toys
* allows exploration of books and how they work – opening covers, turning pages of board books, cloth books and foam bath books
* enhances listening skills
* activates areas of the brain in readiness for learning to read.

Sharing books between 1–3 years (includes points for 0–12 months):

* fosters a love of reading
* develops appropriate book-handling skills: opening the cover, turning pages, and starting at the beginning and progressing to the end

* develops understanding that print represents spoken words
* exposes children to the written language in books, which is different to how we speak
* fosters an awareness that in the English language print is read from left to right.
* encourages basic understandings of story structure: a beginning, middle and end
* develops recognition of story patterns: predictable repetition, rhyming, rhythm of stories
* enhances understanding that print and illustrations work together to tell a story
* builds and enriches vocabulary.

Sharing books between 3–5 years (includes points from 0–3 years):

* gives them basic phonological and alphabet knowledge: that letters make up words, that sounds can be represented by these letters, sensitivity to rhyming words and words that start with the same letter or end with the same letter
* introduces a wide variety of experiences, adventures and worlds, and can also reflect a familiar world – visits to the doctor, bedtime, bathtime, routines, play, starting preschool or school
* fires up the imagination
* helps with problem-solving skills
* develops social and emotional skills.

For the purpose of this example, I am imagining this child is not quite five and has seen Jeanette Rowe's Guess *What? Colours* some years earlier. The various reading skills used are included in brackets. Each double-page spread in the book has two lift-the-flaps.

Cover

Child: I remember this book, I think!

Adult: Do you? What do you think it's about?

Child: I think it's about all the colours?

Adult: Oh, tell me more.

Child: The caterpillar is lots of colours. It's about all those colours, I think.

Adult: I think you might be right. Do you know any of the words on the cover?

Child: I think that one says 'colours'. (Points to **colours**.)

Adult: What makes you say that?

Child: Every letter is a different colour and it starts with 'c' for 'colour'. (Using picture cues and letter/sound knowledge.)

Adult: You're right! That's what that word says. Can you name some colours that you're wearing right now? (Drawing on the child's prior knowledge of the book content.)

Child: I'm wearing a red shirt, blue and black shorts and green sandals.

Adult: Right again! Let's read the cover and get going.

Now read the title and the author name, pointing to each word as you do. Then read aloud the back-cover blurb and confirm or revise your child's predictions about the book.

Page 1

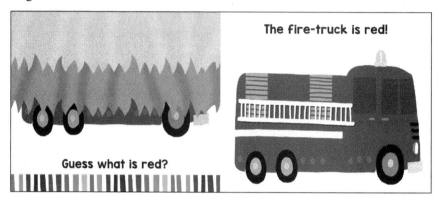

Read aloud the sentence and ask your child to guess what might be red; by doing this you can check their understanding of the text. Now have your child lift the flap. At this point, your child might say, 'The fire-truck!' Agree with them. Then point to the sentence and read it aloud. You are acknowledging that they are correct and then you show them exactly what the text says.

Page 2

This time, read aloud the first three words of the sentence, pointing as you go. Ask your child to supply the last word – the colour word. If they say green, say something like, 'Ooh, let's see.' By involving them in this way, you are highlighting the predictive pattern of the text, and validating their suggestions.

Now have your child lift the flap. Confirm or revise their colour prediction and ask them what the animal is. They might say that it's a shark, a fish or a whale. Nod and read the sentence. If they suggested green rather than blue, at this point you might want to close the flap again and draw their attention to the nose of the whale. Showing them how to use picture clues helps them predict the text.

Page 3

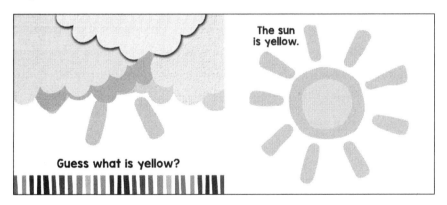

Point to the word 'yellow' and ask your child what they think this word says. If they say yellow, confirm that they are correct. By doing this, you are not only teaching them the word 'yellow' but also highlighting the predictive pattern of the text. They now know the last word in these sentences is the name of a colour.

Invite them to read the sentence with you, having *them* point to each word as they do. Before they open the flap, ask them to list as many yellow things as they can, then ask what they think might be under there. Now encourage them to read this sentence, pointing to each word as they do.

Page 4

Do this page totally uninterrupted, with you reading aloud the sentence, your child opening the flap and you reading the sentence underneath the flap. Now invite your child to do the same, uninterrupted. Doing this will confirm whether your child has picked up the repetitive pattern of the predictive text accurately.

Page 5

If you think your child is ready, encourage them to read the text, open the flap and read what's underneath on their own. If they get the gist right but perhaps say a word or two that didn't quite match the text, congratulate them and tell them it's your turn.

If they called the tractor a car or a truck, think aloud when you come to that word and show them the process that helped you arrive at the word 'tractor'. By doing this, you are allowing them to have a go in a non-threatening way, modelling what good readers do, consolidating the predictive text pattern for them, and reading the correct words aloud.

Pages 6–11
The book continues in the same fashion. Work through each page together as established or, if your child is ready, allow them to read these pages to you.

Page 12

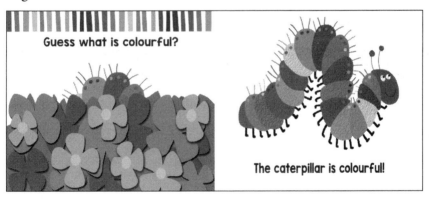

Guess what is colourful?

The caterpillar is colourful!

You might want to signal that something is different about this page by asking what colours they can see. Now read the sentence and ask them what they think might be colourful. Have them open the flap to see what it is and read this sentence aloud.

At the end of the reading, ask your child if they'd like to read the story to you from beginning to end. They will feel a great sense of accomplishment when they do. The more often they revisit the book to read it for themselves, the better. Every time they will be committing words to memory, and with each read, they will read more fluently.

In the blue corner: systematic phonics instruction

The explicit, systematic teaching of phonics has been debated for several decades, just as the whole-language approach has, and phonics has swung in and out of favour. For a few decades when the world turned its back on phonics, it felt as though we threw the baby out with the bathwater, and I'm incredibly relieved to see its recent comeback.

Put simply, phonics is the teaching of the sounds that are made by individual letters or letter groups. For example, the sound for 'd' as in 'dog' or the sound for 'igh' as in 'high'.

It is **explicit** in that children are taught each sound/letter or sound/letters relationship directly, rather than expecting them to learn this knowledge incidentally or when the opportunity arises.

It is **systematic** in that each lesson builds on the last, beginning with simple sound/letter correspondences and rules and progressing through carefully levelled and more complex sound/letter/letters correspondences. Early readers and writers then use this knowledge of sound/letter correspondences to read words and to spell and write them.

Of the seven super skills, phonics instruction covers the first, second, third and fourth.

It's almost an even split between the two approaches, with phonics and whole language each covering different items on the list. Some would even argue that each side addresses all seven to some degree, but 'degree' is the key word in that argument. There is simply no way, for example, that phonics can be taught as thoroughly, explicitly and systematically when it is embedded in lots of other reading methodologies and not given direct teaching time.

Why is this method important for your Gen A child?

When children have a solid knowledge of phonics – sound/letter correspondences – they are able to decode letters and letter blends into their sounds, thus allowing them to read unfamiliar words: a very critical reading skill.

I used this cooking metaphor earlier to explain why you'd use rich texts and books: if you wanted to cook the most show-stopping Peking duck for your guests, would you source a quality recipe or a one-star rated version? Well, the same applies for the teaching of phonics: if you only used half the ingredients and skipped some of the steps, it wouldn't be much good.

Let's put it to the test. When was the last time was you were challenged with having to read an unknown word? Try reading this:

sphenopalatine ganglioneuralgia

How did you do? Were you aware of what you were doing to try to read it? And do you know what it means?

Most of us would have used our knowledge of letter/sound relationships first up. What you might not have noticed is that you probably did a few things at once. Let's use the first word and I'll show you what I did.

1. I knew it started with the *s* sound. I used sound/letter knowledge.
2. I automatically registered that 'ph' when together makes the *f* sound.

3. Once I had the initial sound, I quickly read 'sphen'. Although I wasn't sure whether the 'e' should be pronounced *e* as in 'egg' or *ee* as in 'bean', I opted for the latter – a completely random choice.

4. Next, I thought the 'o' could be pronounced long *o* as in 'glow' or short *o* as in 'off'. I went with *o* as in 'glow'.

5. I did 'palat' automatically, not by sounding out each letter and blending them.

6. For the final three letters, 'ine' could be *ine* as in 'mine' or *een* as in 'Christine'. I chose to go with the sound blend in 'Christine'.

Then, of course, I googled its pronunciation to check how I did! Surprisingly, I got it right; my loosely educated guesses paid off. I relied totally on phonics instruction to read this word, and without it, I don't think I would have made it to first base. Virtually every word a beginning reader sees is an unknown word, just like these ones were to me. How are they to get to first base without any phonics knowledge?

But what do the words mean?

Okay, now you know I can decode, but I still don't know what the words mean. Seeing these words out of context, I had absolutely no hope of knowing either. I'd decoded brilliantly but I'd gained no meaning. Had it been within a sentence, I would have used all my whole-language skill set to work it out: I would have looked at the information I'd read around it, looked for picture clues in any accompanying diagrams, read over the sentence again, read on to the end of the sentence to see what would make sense, and so on.

But I didn't have access to any of that, so I fell back on word parts and word knowledge. I broke it down into smaller words to see if I could make some sense of it. Another valuable reading skill! Looking at the second word, I knew that a ganglion was a cyst that you can get over a joint or a tendon and that neuralgia was a kind of nerve pain. So, I decided the whole term probably meant a growth in your 'spheno' that was causing nerve pain. But what was a spheno? I had absolutely no idea!

Apparently, we have a sphenoid bone in the middle of our skulls. I should have known this because I had a mass in my sphenoid sinus in my thirties that required surgery. Funnily enough, during diagnosis and management I didn't ever see the word written down and the whole thing was obviously traumatic enough for me to bury it deep down in my memory. So for those of you, like me, who don't know what the words mean, no, it isn't a growth on your sphenoid bone causing nerve pain. That would make sense, wouldn't it? Too much sense for medicine. It's actually the medical term for an ice-cream headache!

So you can see, phonics is extremely important because it is the foundation for beginning to read. Children need it to build up a bank of words that they sound out at first, but over time learn to read by sight. As they progress, the process becomes automatic and speedy. Once they're speedy and in this zone, they can move on and read all kinds of things using a combination of whole-language principles and a suite of reading skills, relying only on phonics when they come to an unfamiliar word.

But you can also see that as children move from a strong phonics base, they need lots of other reading skills to progress. Later, they will need to be able to comprehend what they are reading well so that they'll be able to do other things like:

* identify the main idea in a text
* synthesise information and put it into their own words
* compare and contrast

* problem-solve
* draw conclusions about what they've read
* draw on background knowledge
* 'read between the lines' or 'pick up clues' as they read to infer what's really happening.

And this is just a short list of things they'll need to do, which is why I believe it should all be taught and not just one or another approach.

Synthetic phonics: the new kid on the phonics block you need to know about

Learning to read and spell English isn't easy. There are so many exceptions to the rules to stumble on. But what if you learnt how to spell the words at the same time as you learnt to read them?

Research shows that learning this way avoids lots of roadblocks, and it is best learnt with synthetic phonics. It's like the superhero version of phonics and is quick, hugely successful and a game changer for early reading and writing. You want a piece of synthetic phonics action for your child. Trust me on this!

What is synthetic phonics?

Synthetic phonics is a method of teaching your child reading and spelling at the same time, rather than separately. It helps your child learn to blend sounds to read a word. And in reverse, they can separate or segment sounds and blends to spell a word. If your child can sound out a word, they can read it and spell it! It makes a lot of sense, doesn't it?

With synthetic phonics, children learn the speech sounds for the letters (called *phonemes*) and the groups of letters that represent

BLENDING TO READ

SEGMENTING TO SPELL

those sounds (called *graphemes*), just like any phonics program. There are three key things to remember:

* A single sound (*phoneme*) can be represented by one, two, three or four different letters. For example, the phoneme / s / is spelled using a single 's' in 'sat' and two 'ss' in 'glass'.

* A single sound (*phoneme*) can also be represented by different spellings (*graphemes*). For example, the sound / c / can be spelled using the letter 'c' as in 'cat' and using the letter 'k' as in 'kite'.

* One spelling (*grapheme*) can represent multiple sounds (*phonemes*). For example, the spelling 'ea' can be pronounced with short *e* as in 'bread' and long *ee* as in 'bead'.

How is it different from other analytical phonics programs?

There are multiple differences between the old form of 'analytical' phonics and the new 'synthetic' phonics. I've summarised the big differences in the following table.

Analytical phonics	Synthetic phonics
Sounds are taught individually.	Groups of sounds are taught at the same time for quicker learning.
The focus is on the initial sound and word families.	The focus is on all the sounds in a word, so it's much more holistic.
Spelling is taught independently from reading.	Reading and spelling are taught at the same time. If you can read a word using synthetic phonics, then you can already spell it as well.
The focus is on the 26 letters of the alphabet and their corresponding sounds.	Children are taught the 44 phonemes of the English language and how these phonemes can be spelt.
Sounds are taught with picture clues.	Learning is focused on the sounds and blends, not on picture clues, which will not always be there, and not guessing.

Why is this method important for your Gen A child?

Well, because research shows that all children benefit from learning via synthetic phonics, and quickly! Out of the two main types of phonics instruction – analytical and synthetic – synthetic phonics has been shown to be more successful in helping children learn to read and spell, and that's what you want for your child.

A large-scale study of more than 270,000 students throughout the UK that assessed initial learning and its impact four years down the track found that this form of learning has large benefits for all students at ages five to seven, and that at age seven, those taught to read using other methods were behind those using synthetic phonics.[2]

Using this method offers a faster-paced way to learn reading and writing through progressive stages that match children's learning-development phases. It is a much more comprehensive system than analytical phonics and allows them to advance their reading, spelling and writing in tandem. It also equips children with the tools to sound, read and spell out new words that they haven't come across before, rather than just memorising words. Their reading and writing development will soar right before your eyes.

Why is it so successful?

The key is that a child is never asked to read or spell anything they don't already know how to blend or segment. For example, a five-year-old might learn the sounds for the letters *s*, *a*, *t*, *p*, *i* and *n*. Then, words using these sounds are used to make decodable books that your child can read. When they learn the next batch of sounds, these and the new sounds are used to generate a bigger pool of decodable words that are used in new decodable books. And on it goes. At the same time, they will be learning to segment these words to spell and write. The reading, writing and spelling all happen at the same time.

Of course, there are words that cannot be phonetically blended and segmented because they don't follow the usual letter/sound correspondences. The word 'to', for example, is a word that must be learned by sight. However, research shows that despite the 'o' in 'to' being tricky (they will want it to sound like the short *o* for 'orange'), children will still sound out the 't' and guess the word correctly enough times to learn it. So, phonic knowledge helps even in the tricky cases.

Books and activities for children that work on synthetic-phonics principles build on a combination of learned sounds and a levelled sight-word list that grows alongside the sounds. Once a child knows these, they can read them and write them, and that gives them a huge rush of success, making them want to read and write more.

Let me show you how to share a decodable book with your child, and at the same time you'll be able to see clearly how synthetic phonics works for blending to read. You will also be able to see how different this process is to sharing a book using a whole-language approach. I'm using my book *The Tent*, part of Lake Press's Whiz Kids Kits.

Look at the front cover of *The Tent* together and ask your child to read the title. Help them by blending sounds together to read the words if they struggle. Now, look at the illustration and ask them what they think the book will be about.

These are the new sounds and sight words that your child will have already learnt if they are up to this book. All these sounds and new sight words will be used in its pages. Review them together and have your child practise reading all the sight words accurately before you begin to read. This will help them to read the book more fluently and make the whole experience more pleasurable and successful.

Here are the sounds and sight words your child will have learnt previously in earlier books. Some of them will be used in this book for revision. Review them together.

In which we meet the sounds and letters:
ff, ll, ss, zz
And the sight words:
who, she, put, and, go.

And revise the sounds and letters:
s a t m p l n d g o c h b e k f r u l j v w y z
And the sight words:
the, was, he, on, a, has, of, is, my, no

If your child stumbles on the sight words 'and' and 'put', have them point to each and tell them the words. These words will be used again and again so that your child has plenty of opportunities to learn and practise them.

Tess and Fuzz put beds in the tent.

If your child struggles to read an unfamiliar decodable word, ask them to place their finger below each letter and say the sound for it. Then help them to blend the sounds together to read the word.

Tess puts a bus in the tent.

She puts a doll in the tent.

The pattern of the text should help with the reading now. However, if there is a decodable word that they do not know, sound out and blend the word together rather than telling them the word.

Your child might struggle with the sight word 'who'. If they don't remember it, ask them to read on to the end of the sentence and point out the question mark at the end. If they still don't know the word, tell them. They will have time to get it right in the next read-through.

They should have no problems reading this page. At the end of the reading, ask your child some questions to check their comprehension and to encourage interaction and reflection. Then ask them to read the book to you again. In doing so, they will build reading fluency, consolidate their learning and give themselves a massive confidence boost. They really can read!

A big mess!

Levelled readers and decodable books

Most schools will send levelled school readers home for your child to help them with learning to read. These books are not decodable phonic-based books. They are levelled by reading difficulty, sentence length and word count, and usually belong to a large literacy program that the school is using. Your child's teacher will know what level your child is at and when they need to progress to the next level.

For children who take to the whole-language approach for learning to read and have some knowledge of phonics, they will learn to read these levelled readers, and will progress through the various levels. These are the children who will learn to read no matter what.

For many children at the beginning of their learning-to-read journey, these books will be hard, and they may have little success with them. In turn, they'll likely become frustrated and turned off by their early lack of success.

At the very early stages of learning to read, synthetic phonics–based books coupled with solid teaching are extremely effective. Read and share beautiful story or picture books with your child to instil a love of books, but when they are beginning to actually learn to read, be sure to include synthetic phonics–decodable books in your reading materials. It's these they will have most success with in the early stages of their literacy learning. And for children finding learning to read a challenge, decodable books and a solid base of synthetic-phonics instruction are an absolute must.

Likewise, if you find your child is struggling with the levelled readers that come home in their schoolbag, get them onto decodable books as quickly as you can. More and more schools are coming on board with synthetic phonics and will have books that your child can bring home. Public libraries are also beginning to stock them, as are bookstores and department stores.

Here are some titles and sources worth investigating:

* littlelearnersloveliteracy.com.au
* Spelfabet First Phonics Picture Book (free download from spelfabet.com.au)
* getreadingright.com.au
* Andy Griffiths' rhyming stories for beginning readers, such as *The Cat on the Mat Is Flat*, *Frog on a Log in a Bog* and *Duck in a Truck in the Muck*
* My own Synthetic Phonics kits: Stages 1, 2 and 3, and Whiz Kids Reading Fun: Synthetic Phonics Kits (three decodable readers per kit)

Once your child is reading decodables fluently, it's important to move them quickly on to quality, natural-language picture books where the reading environments are carefully controlled to ensure success. These books will give your child the satisfying, rich and engaging read they'll want, and will help them develop fluency and a real love of reading. When children are reading what they love, they'll want to read more and will go from strength to strength at an astonishing rate.

Where to from here?

Okay, so we know children need quality books. And as they continue on their reading journey, they need books that absorb them. They need books that are virtually unputdownable. They need to read books, and lots of them. They will still need to be read to, and to share reading with you right through their primary years, as well as reading silently on their own.

So, what are the best books for your child and how can you be sure you get the match between reader and book right? Let's move on and find out!

To see my top trade early readers and chapter books and my top phonics-based resources, head to the 7 Steps section of my website.

Takeaways from this chapter

Children need to be exposed to as many reading techniques as possible so that they develop a suite of skills they can use. Therefore, they need exposure to both whole language and phonics approaches because:

* Many children will struggle to learn to read without solid phonics instruction in the early years.

* Whole-language philosophies bring with them a suite of skills that children will need to draw on alongside phonics in the early years, and more so as they move through the primary years.
* Rich, quality books offer a wealth of layered experiences that decodable books cannot. However, many children beginning to read will need to learn with decodable materials.
* Both sides address the super skills for reading.

Synthetic phonics is important for your Gen A child because:

* It teaches reading, spelling and writing at the same time – if you can blend sounds together to read a word, you can segment those sounds to spell and write the word.
* It is a fast, intuitive, success-based method of learning to read and write.
* It is backed by research and studies over several years and is proven to be the most effective of any early reading program.

When thinking about reading materials, remember:

* Levelled readers are not for everyone in the early years!
* If, as a beginner reader, your child thrives from a phonics approach, get them reading with decodable books, not levelled readers.
* If, as an early reader, your child is struggling to learn to read, get them into a synthetic-phonics program and onto decodable books.
* Once a child has a solid foundation of sounds and blending skills and a suite of words they know by sight, move them from decodable books to quality story and picture books as quickly as you can.
* Keep reading to and with your child right through primary school.
* Foster the love of reading at home. Make it as special, pleasurable and as success-oriented as you can.

'There is no such thing as a kid who hates reading.

There are kids who love reading, and kids who are reading the wrong books.'

— JAMES PATTERSON

Step 7:

Finding just-right books for any age

The author-signing area at this very well-known writers festival is super-organised. As children line up with their parents, they are encouraged to doodle on a papered wall or write sticky notes about their day that they can also stick on the wall. The children are animated and excited. They're all chatting as though they've known each other longer than just the amount of time they've stood together in this queue. It makes me smile. And then I am snapped back to my job at the table, not by a child but by a parent's voice.

The child is not quite with me yet. He is next in line. The parent is telling him that the book he wants is not for him, and I'm immediately intrigued. Admittedly, I have several series on the table and they cater for different interests. I wonder what it is he wants that his parent thinks is wrong for him. When they reach me, the parent grabs a *Zac Power Spy Recruit* bind-up and tells the child that this is perfect, that he will love it. And that may well be so. But the child grabs a copy of *Harriet Clare Mystery Dare* from the pile and says that this is the book he wants; he says that he wants to solve the mystery at the caves just like the Jenolan Caves where they've been to; says he thinks he can help Ethan and Harriet catch the thief that stole the special tortoiseshell mermaid comb; he wants to read about the secret tunnels to the caves.

I am devastated at what takes place next; wholly devastated and not surprised, simultaneously.

I smile at the boy and say that I think he will help immensely in solving everything in this book, *Mystery Dare*, and that the characters need his help, for sure. The parent, however, says that the book has a girl dressed as a detective on the cover and that the child needs a book with a boy as the main character – he is a boy, after all. I manage to say, 'Oh,' as I have a total Nina moment from the show *Offspring*. Like her, my head wrestles all at once with:

A: If I tell them that it's actually really good that boys read books with female main characters, just as girls read books with male main characters all the time, and start sprouting about all the reasons why this is a good thing, am I undermining the parent in front of the child?

B: Should I point out that there are girls and boys in most of my books and that they are from different cultural heritages, and would that even remotely help at all, even though I know it should?

C: If I tell them about how important it is for a child to actually choose what they want to read, will I get right up this person's nose?

My Nina moment passes and I boldly (way more boldly than I feel) gaze at the parent and calmly say that I feel so happy they've raised such an awesome child – one who wants to read from a number of perspectives, who wants to explore a story for all its worth, and who will have empathy and insight with all people, not just himself, and more importantly as he grows, not just with males. (I hold my tongue from adding that our domestic violence rate against women is scary, and that I believe change can only happen if we think about how we raise our boys from the cradle up, and how reading diversely can make a significant contribution to this.)

I need to tell you that this story ended badly. The parent gave me a smile, looked very chuffed, chest puffed like a peacock, then thrust a book with a male main character on the cover in front of me to sign. I longed to sneak a copy of *Harriet Clare Mystery Dare*, for free, under the little boy's arm as he went, but I had no opportunity. I was devastated indeed.

And so this chapter starts with reading diversely, followed by book choice – two essential elements (but not all) in the process of matching your Gen A child with just the right books.

Reading diversity

Girls will read books starring boys but boys will not read books starring girls. In my fifteen years of touring and presenting in schools as a children's author, I thought I'd heard every version of this gender disparity regarding books. Then I came across an interview with Shannon

Hale, a bestselling children's author who writes books predominately with female main characters. She was invited to speak at a school and when she arrived in the hall, she found that all the boys had been excused from the event. I don't think I will ever get over this, and I'm relieved to say that it has never happened to me. But has it really come to this? I'm sure that when a male writer arrives with his male main characters in tow, the girls will not be excused: they'll be expected not only to listen and enjoy the presentation but to contribute as well. So, girls are expected to read books with boys in them. Teachers read aloud books about boys to mixed groups all the time. People with different cultural heritages read books filled with white-skinned characters. Yet boys are excused from reading books with girls cast in the main role. Why?

I grew up reading widely and still do. I don't think twice about reading a book with male characters, possibly because as I was growing up, most of the books presented to me had males cast in the lead. But what are we teaching our boys when we discourage them from reading a book from a female perspective? What messages are we sending to our girls when they are expected to read books with males in them, but boys are excused from reading books with girls in them and from hearing a female author talk about her writing?

These are the dangerous messages we drive home to our young readers each and every time this gender bias is reinforced:

* Books with girls are lesser and not as important.
* Stories with girls are boring, unappealing and not engaging.
* Boys only need to relate to boys but girls need to relate to everyone.
* Girls are automatically readers who can read anything, but boys need to be given special care, attention and carefully curated reading material to make them readers.

* Boys are the heroes in all the stories, while girls just need to enjoy the story, whether they are heroines in it or not.
* Boys' stories are universal while girls' stories are only for girls.

Don't ask if it is a girl book or a boy book, but if it is a *good* book

Interestingly, it's often not the kids who seem to have an issue with this, as my opening anecdote shows. I spend more than a third of every year in schools and at festivals presenting to children, and I regularly ask my groups what they like to read. I get all kinds of answers that include things like funny books, books with big issues to solve, books about dragons, mysteries, adventures, and stories about everyday problems and situations. What I have never, ever been told is, 'I like books about boys,' or 'I like books about girls.'

The reality is that what all children like is a really good read! They like books that transport them to other worlds and keep them there, that grab their attention and captivate their imagination, that are compelling and hard to put down. When they're in the grip of a thrilling tale, they actually don't care what gender the main character is, as long as they are a believable character that resonates.

It's not the kids who seem to have an issue getting out in the playground and playing in mixed groups, in creating plays that cast all genders in key roles, in collaborating in their story-writing to do the same. While they may differ in some interests, kids have no trouble coming together. Why suggest that it should be any different when they come to losing themselves in the wonderful world of a book?

It's not all about the cover

Yes, I know, it's easy for me to write that when you're the ones going into a bookshop and being confronted by loads of glittery pink covers with girls in frilly dresses, make-up and sparkly accessories, or stacks of boys doing something adventurous against a wild background. But I urge you to look further, and not just past these run-of-the mill covers to the others: look *inside* all the covers to see what really lies between them.

When you're next selecting books with your child, try focusing on these things:

* Consider their interests and what they'd like to know more about, what sparks their imagination or just what they feel like reading at the time. We all have different reading moods. I go through patches of crime, then I want World War I and II stories, and then I feel like escaping into some fantasy. I'm forever changing, and children do so even more.
* Help expand their understanding and empathy by helping them find books about people who are different from them. Engage them on a whole new level.
* Look for characters who have incredible journeys, who are challenged, who are resourceful, resilient and strong, and who take your child to new ways of being and thinking.
* Be mindful of books that cast monsters and baddies as only male.
* Hunt out those books that you know your child will find a compelling, romping good read regardless of the gender of the main character.

What do children gain from reading diversely?

The thing about us humans is that we trade in stories. It's what we do. Think about it: when you meet a friend for coffee, you exchange stories about what's happening in your workplace, some drama playing out in the extended family, a breakup and why it happened, or a funny story about something your child did. It's our currency. It's how we form bonds. We swap personal and not-so-personal stories all the time.

How we respond, relate and reflect on those stories and anecdotes cements those bonds and relationships – or it whittles them away. These skills – the responding, relating, the understanding – most of us take for granted, but they are among the most important things we need to teach our children. And that's where reading fiction can work wonders. It's just another good reason to ensure we raise readers.

> *'There has been an extraordinary shift . . . A concept*
> *that has been buried in psychology textbooks for nearly*
> *a century – empathy – is coming to be seen as one of the*
> *fundamental forces for tackling global challenges.'*[1]
>
> **ROMAN KRZNARIC**

Researchers have finally documented what we've all known for ages – that reading fiction from different perspectives improves a reader's capacity to understand what others are thinking and feeling: that exact thing that helps us form bonds and build healthy, worthwhile relationships. And specifically, reading fiction that portrays dynamic characters who grow, change and develop emotionally and socially: fiction that explores the psychology of characters, their relationships, their motivations and actions, their emotions, their vulnerabilities, their flaws, warts and all.

Narratives where main characters' minds are not fully formed but rather 'works in progress' provide opportunity for readers to fill in the gaps: to reflect on characters' feelings, emotions, intentions and actions. They pull readers into their world and get them to walk in their shoes, their minds, their hearts. This interaction and awareness stays with the reader long after the story's end and goes with them into the real world, supporting them in their interactions with real children, and in later life with adults. These characters can teach readers vital values and understandings about social and emotional behaviour.

Fiction really does allow the reader to experience the world from another person's point of view. It helps children develop empathy – a critical skill for the new world that Gen A children will inhabit. It is Gen A who are most at risk of missing out on developing it due to the enormous amounts of time they'll spend in the shallowly connected online world of social media.[2]

So, we are seriously letting our boys down if we don't encourage them to read books with girls as main characters. We are letting our girls down if we don't let them see that girls can be heroes too, and that boys enjoy seeing that just as much as when males are cast in the lead role.

I'm not saying that's all they should read. Of course, girls will read books starring girls and boys will read books starring boys, and that's a good thing. What I am saying is that all children need exposure to stories from different points of view as well. They need books that don't perpetuate this gender bias, and not a whole diet of books that do.

These children will grow to be adults. The messages we send as they grow are critical, and have a huge role to play in the types of adults they will become. Let's build a generation of empathetic human beings, and let's use reading and books to help do that.

*'When I think about how I understand my role as a
citizen, setting aside being president, and the most
important set of understandings that I bring to that
position of citizen, the most important stuff I've
learned I think I've learned from novels.
It has to do with empathy. It has to do with being
comfortable with the notion that the world is
complicated and full of grays, but there's still truth
there to be found, and that you have to strive for that
and work for that. And the notion that it's possible to
connect with some[one] else even though they're very
different from you.'*[4]

– BARACK OBAMA

Seeing yourself in a book

Can anything be more important? I think not. In the 1980s, I was reading a book about fairies to my kindergarten class in the western suburbs of Sydney. A student asked why there weren't any black fairies in it. I had a small number of Indigenous students in the class and this question made me feel like I'd failed them. Why indeed were there no black fairies? What could I possibly answer?

And now I think, what if these children walked through life never seeing themselves represented anywhere in the books that surrounded them? How must it feel for any child to see a constant parade of characters who don't look like them?

Our world is culturally diverse. Classrooms are filled with children from diverse backgrounds. Children need access to books that reflect this cultural diversity. It's vitally important that they see themselves in some books – it tells them that their cultural identity is important, that their traditions and stories are important, that they are important. And when children see themselves in books, it makes reading more inclusive and enjoyable.

In times gone by, it was incredibly hard to find quality children's books written by people from different cultural backgrounds. And when most of the books out there feature white characters telling white stories, it offers an inaccurate image of what it is to be human. Much is being done to close this gap and things are better now, though we still have a way to go. To find culturally diverse books for your child, search the Cultural Diversity Database[3] at the National Centre for Australian Children's Literature. You can search using key terms such as cultural identity, traditions, migration and language. This site is a work in progress and more books are being added all the time so try to revisit it from time to time.

Five tips for exposing your child to diversity in books

Help your child find appealing books that have:

* main characters who are from varying cultures and ethnicities
* illustrations that reflect a diverse society – for example, a group of characters from varying backgrounds doing things; not always showing Mum in the kitchen and Dad at work
* engaging, well-crafted stories
* stories told from a different point of view than their own
* authors and illustrators from a variety of cultures and ethnicities telling their own stories in their own authentic voice.

Letting your child choose their own books

When I'm in the market for a new book, I browse the bookshop shelves, I make a shortlist pile, I ask the booksellers what they think and if they have any recommendations based on the types of things I like to read, or I ask for something completely fresh and different that they think I might love. I read all the cover blurbs; I might even read some reviews or recommendations online before I hit the bookshop. Sometimes I'll try a sample chapter on Kindle. Sometimes I'll read a dozen different sample chapters before I settle on something I want to continue with. What I don't do is stand back and wait to be told what I must read and what I must buy and allow the choosing to be done by someone else entirely.

Retaining the power of choice ensures that I'm 99.9 per cent on target for getting a book I will enjoy reading – and that's what I want. Yes, I garner opinions. Yes, I sift through the books and choose carefully, as I sometimes take those opinions on board and other times I dismiss them. I like asking for some guidance, but at the end of the day, what I walk out of that store with is my choice and my choice alone.

We want to raise readers who can do exactly this. And to do that, we have to start that process early.

Giving children power to choose their books is the key to raising readers who will read for the sheer enjoyment of it. It won't be a chore. And we all know that the more this happens, the better their reading and writing will become.

However, letting them at it completely unguided will most likely yield less-than-perfect results. I suggest you enhance their decision-making with a little guidance, just like the guidance we seek when choosing a book for ourselves. After that guidance has been offered and your child has narrowed down their pile themselves, let them make the final choice.

Children should be involved with this process from a young age. They can begin to browse books as soon as they can handle them without causing damage, and as they grow, their ability to choose a book for themselves that they will really enjoy will grow too.

☀ FACT

Ninety-one per cent of children aged six to eighteen surveyed in the Scholastic Kids & Family Reading Report said, 'My favourite books are the ones that I have picked out myself.'[5]

Why children should choose their own books

* When you give children the opportunity to make their own informed choices about what to read, you are empowering them and giving them more ownership in the process, and in turn they're investing in their choices.

* When children are allowed to make the decisions, they'll take risks and explore more books in their curating and culling process than they'd normally come across.

* Children who choose their own books will begin to talk about books with their friends to find out what they're reading. They'll want to know what they thought was good and why, and they'll give their own recommendations in return. This, in turn, raises reading in their eyes as a worthwhile and cool thing to do. Their conversations won't just be about games or online activities. Books will begin to compete, and that's a really good thing.

* When children choose their own books, they'll have positive experiences with books and will therefore read more. The more they read, the better their reading and writing will become.

* Children choosing their own books are more likely to read from a variety of perspectives, which helps develop empathy and inclusion.

A study on book choice

A University of Rochester (New York) experiment looked at the impact of children choosing their own reading materials. Eighteen students in grades K–2 were allowed to pick thirteen books to read over the summer. The rest of their classmates were prescribed what they must read. Reading levels were tested before and after, with the students who choose their own books significantly outstripping those in the other group.[6]

Enhancing book choice

It's pretty clear that much of early reading success is about confidence and enjoyment. If children enjoy reading and feel that they can do it, then they'll keep doing it – and when children keep reading, their confidence and their reading enjoyment soar. But what if a book is too easy or too hard?

Too easy?

Well, that depends on the purpose for reading, and how often the books your child chooses are too easy. Firstly, there's no such thing as an easy book if your child is reading it for pleasure, and not every book your child reads needs to extend their reading level. What's important is that they enjoy it.

If, on the other hand, all they *ever* read are books that are too easy for them, their reading vocabulary won't grow, and they won't be challenged. Try not to worry about this too much, though, because they will be challenged with harder and harder reading material at school.

There is much to be gained from your child reading books in their comfort zone.

* Because they'll find the reading level less of a challenge, their minds are freer to focus on the events in the story and comprehend and reflect on them in a more significant way.
* Easier reads allow children to practise and consolidate their reading skills.
* The more they read, no matter the reading level, the more they'll learn.
* Having an easy read before bedtime can help children relax and prepare for sleep.
* Books in a child's comfort zone make the whole experience incredibly pleasurable and rewarding, and therefore are very good for their self-esteem and their opinion of themselves as a capable reader.

Too hard?

A diet of books that are just too hard is a different story altogether, pardon the pun! If a book has too many hard words, children will stumble through the story, continually stopping to tackle tricky vocabulary. When this happens too much, children begin to lose the thread and the meaning of the story. When they start to lose the meaning, their attention wanders. Before you know it, the book has been put down; the chances of it being picked up again are incredibly slim.

If the books your child is reading are constantly too hard, it will turn them off the whole process very quickly. They'll begin to see themselves as a hopeless reader, and so they'll become more and more reluctant to try.

That doesn't mean that because your child can't read a book for themselves, it should be off limits to them. Children who are struggling with actual reading don't have issues with understanding. So if you know a book that they really want to read is too hard for them, read it to them, or use an audiobook version and encourage them to read along as it's being read aloud to them.

That just-right book

When your child is looking for a book to read *independently* that's 'not too easy' as well as 'not so hard that it's out of reach', how can you help them find it?

There are two pieces to the perfect-book puzzle for independent reading:

* a match between content and your child's interests, and
* a match with their reading ability.

When these two things come together, the choice is bang on. Here are some tips that will help you get it right.

Content and interest: find a book your child wants to read

Content is king. If a book's content grabs a child and gets them reading on their own terms, it's gold. So consider what your child is interested in.

What do they do when they're not reading? Their interests and pastimes are often a great place to start when thinking about what books to read. There are books about adventure, sport, beasts, dinosaurs, fairies, everyday problems, friendship struggles, outer space, warriors, computers and many of their favourite TV shows and games. Go to the early-reader section of your bookshop or library and see what's there.

While you're there, judge a book by its cover. In this context, it's fine because the covers are designed to help you know what kind of story is inside. Here's how you can guide your child to choose the right book for them:

* Have them pick covers they like the look of, regardless of pre-dominant colours and whether they have a girl or boy in the main illustration.
* Have them read the back-cover blurb and ask if it appeals to them.
* Then ask them to revisit the cover armed with that information to see if they think it's still a good match.
* Lastly, look inside together. The interior of the book, its layout and its design are even more important. Is the type size appropriate for your child's age and ability? Are there lots of small and manageable chapters to foster a sense of achievement? Are there engaging illustrations that provide reading breaks? Be sure to consider the number of words on each page, too.

Readability: find a book your child can read

The ideal match between a reader and a text is a book that is perfectly pitched to give a child reading confidence as they build their literacy skills: a book that they can read with about 90 per cent accuracy.

Anything harder will most likely turn them off reading. One new word in every ten words ensures their comprehension and enjoyment, and further builds their literacy skills and vocabulary.

The 'five finger rule' is one of the quickest and easiest ways to gauge whether a book is too hard. When you find a book that your child wants to read, ask them to start reading a page aloud. If they stumble over a word, hold up a finger. Keep adding a finger for every word they find tricky. If five fingers are up by the end of the page, the child has spent more time concentrating on difficult words than on reading the story and they will have lost track of the storyline of the book. The book is too hard, at least for now.

Use this table as a rough guide to help you and your child assess books. It works for beginner, struggling, competent and enthusiastic readers.

	Beginner and struggling readers	Competent and enthusiastic readers
Length	* one line of text per page to a few lines of text per page, with fewer words * 16–60 pages	* full pages of text with paragraphs and larger numbers of words * 60 pages and beyond
Words	* mostly high frequency words, familiar words * fewer words per sentence * easily solved words with familiar spelling patterns	* texts with many topic-related and 'interest' words * varied sentence lengths * complex words solved using a variety of reading strategies

	Beginner and struggling readers	Competent and enthusiastic readers
Print	* larger font size * clear, legible font * greater space between words and lines	* increasingly smaller font size * spacing between words and lines becoming smaller and more standard
Illustrations	* illustrations on every or almost every page * illustrations that support the text and give clues to the meaning of the text	* fewer illustrations to no illustrations at all * where illustrations are used, they extend the text rather than supporting the reading of less familiar words
Content	* 'everyday' stories and familiar themes * predictable story structure with a simple problem and solution * simple ideas * straightforward plots * topics the reader has experience of	* more complex ideas, unfamiliar topics and themes * more complex structure, including flashbacks, time-slips, time shifts, changes in point of view, plot twists, subplots, explicit and implicit ideas

An important word on reading resilience

As I write this book, there is a craze out there: a big smelly farty craze. In fact, there are so many books flooding the market about poos and farts and who knows what else, I wonder how any others can breathe. And then there are the joke books – the funny books with about twenty words per page on them and lots of cartoony illustrations.

These books usually come packaged like a grown-up novel. They're a novel shape, mostly a novel size and a novel thickness – often a few hundred pages in length. But that's where the similarities end. Inside the covers of these books are very low word counts despite their page extents, and they tend to be thinner on plot.

These books are great! I'm not saying they're not. They make readers of lots of children every day. They make children feel like they can actually read a whole book easily, giving them a sense of success and self-esteem. And they make them laugh! I applaud these books. They do their job and do it well.

What concerns me is that some children are reading these books as early as they can and still reading them into their tweens – with not much else in between. Is too much of a good thing bad for your child in this regard? Absolutely!

Let your child read these books if they choose; let them revisit them as many times as they like. But do all you can to move them on when these books have done their job. Your role is to encourage your child to read widely for pleasure: to read books of varying lengths and books that make them think and open their eyes, their hearts and their imaginations. And you need to do this because a child who has grown on a diet of twenty words per page of the funny genre where the balance of the book is cartoons will come a cropper in high school and beyond.

Children need reading resilience. In high school, they will need to read big slabs of text, and it's not always about what they love, find funny or are keenly interested in. They'll be expected to read lengthy novels and analyse and write about them. They won't get to say, 'No, I want to read something else,' after the first page, first paragraph or first chapter. How are they to cope if all they've had is a diet of joke books with small bites of text?

Be a reading role model

Your child idealises you, wants to be you, thinks you know everything there is to know in this world. Use that to your advantage and let them see that you're a reader and that you value reading. It will rub off! Trust me on this.

If you can, set a good example by:

* having reading material of all shapes and sizes in the home: books, magazines, crosswords, instruction manuals, cooking books, newspapers and online texts
* drawing attention to the things you read and sharing some of the appropriate ones with your child
* borrowing books from the library together, as a family
* having reading material on your bedside table, just like your child
* curling up on the lounge or in your favourite spot and reading for leisure. They'll get their books and read with you!

Takeaways from this chapter

* Reading teaches children empathy and understanding.

* Reading diversely allows children to experience other cultures and their stories.

* Children need to read books with girls and boys in the starring role.

* Be aware of the gender bias messages that can be communicated to your child when choosing books to read.

* Find books that are a great read, regardless of cover colours or the gender of the main character.

* Encourage your child to read from a variety of perspectives other than their own.

* Be wary of books that stereotype: Mum as homemaker, Dad always into sport.

* We all need to see ourselves in some of the books we read.

* Let children choose the books they want to read with some guidance from you.

* Children who choose the books they read do better academically and read more.

* Books that are too easy are okay. Just not all the time.

* Books that are too hard are best shared or read aloud.

* Match your child's interests with a book's content as they learn to read. Then widen their reading horizons.

* Match your child's reading ability with a book for independent reading.

* Help your child develop reading resilience, encourage reading growth and move them on from a diet of the same thing all the time.

* Be a reading role model for your child if you can.

And that's a wrap!

You've made it through the seven simple steps guaranteed to get your child reading, done and dusted! At this point, my best parting tip to you is to enjoy every minute of the ride. Make incorporating these steps fun and something everyone looks forward to, and there will be no tears. It doesn't have to be about heavy learning – anything but. If they're engaged, if they want to keep reading, if they're hanging on the edge of their seats wanting to know what happens next, you've won!

Remember, reading happens in its own time. You don't want to miss that magical moment when it comes together for your child and they become a reader. And it will happen if your child has no identified literacy learning problems. If they do have difficulties, however, read on for further advice.

'At the moment when
we persuade a child,
any child, to cross
that magic threshold
into a library, we
change their lives
forever, for the better.'

– BARACK OBAMA

Difficulty learning to read, write and spell

In the first chapter, we looked at what our brains do when we learn to read. I touched on what happens in the brains of children who struggle to master reading or who have dyslexia. And just to recap, I said that a struggling reader is not lazy – far from it! They are not stupid, either. The danger is that they will believe they are if they don't progress or get the help they need before they become disengaged.

Struggling readers who don't get the intervention they need will not get better at reading, and they will fall further and further behind. The sooner that intervention happens, the better. Quite frankly, it's important that parents don't wait until someone else raises the flag. Many children's struggles are picked up and they receive the evaluation and help they need. However, some may never be picked up and these children will struggle through life, never knowing why they have difficulties and what could be done to ease them.

No one wants their child to slip through the net. Teachers do their best, but you're the one who sees your child one on one the most frequently. If you have concerns, discuss them with your child's teacher in the first instance.

Gen Alpha and reading difficulties

Reading, writing and understanding is fundamental for success across every subject area, so it's vital that no child gets left behind. And much can be done to minimise the impact of reading difficulties on a child's literacy journey, particularly in the early years at home, at school and with professionals, if required.

If your child is struggling with learning to read, know that:

* Dyslexia is not an intellectual disability.
* Not all strugglers have a reading disability. Many simply have not developed the reading skills necessary to thrive, for a variety of reasons. They may be labelled with reading difficulties but will soon master the skills needed with tailored, individual, intensive teaching that cannot be given in a crowded classroom.
* Almost always, these children are bright, dedicated and keen to learn. Their brains are simply working in a different way. Once diagnosed, in many cases much of this can be corrected.
* Early assessment and intervention is the key to academic success and happiness.

There are a number of learning difficulties that can impact a child's experiences at school. For the purposes of this book, I'm going to focus on working memory, dyslexia and dysgraphia, as these are the most common difficulties that affect a child's ability to acquire literacy in a struggle-free way.

Working memory

Working memory is where we store information that we know we're going to need to use. It's like the notes app of our brain. Children with poor working memories struggle to grab and store the information they need, and this can wreak havoc when they're trying to master learning to read.

Here's a mild case of poor working memory in action: you make a list of groceries that you need, but when you hit the supermarket you realise you left it at home. You do your best, but when you get home you find you've forgotten several things you needed. Had your working memory been firing on all four cylinders, you would have most likely nailed the shopping without the list.

Working memory problems are one of the biggest issues in reading difficulties. Children need their working memories when reading to:

* read an unknown word
* decode an unknown word
* put information they've read into their own words
* comprehend what they've just read
* problem-solve
* retell and sequence events in a story
* follow a set of instructions
* keep their place on the page.

Could your child have working memory problems?

This checklist will help you identify whether your child might have a weak working memory. It's a guide to the sort of things to look out for.

Answering yes to one or two of these points does not necessarily mean that your child has poor working memory. Some of these points may indicate other learning difficulties such as attention deficit hyperactivity disorder (ADHD), but if you answer yes to several of these points, it's a red flag for working memory and is worth investigating further. A proper diagnosis from a professional is the only way to find out if indeed your child has working memory problems.

* Next time your child wants to tell you something, have them wait until you've finished a task, then ask them to share it with you. Have they forgotten what they wanted to tell you? And does this happen often?

* Does your child have difficulty following a sequence of instructions, such as collecting their sports bag from their room and then collecting the library books that need to be returned from the hallway?

* Does your child constantly lose or forget things?

* Does your child struggle to retell a simple story you've just read to them?

* Does your child forget what they've learned quickly?

* Is your child a big daydreamer and do they appear to be distracted or inattentive on a regular basis?

* Is your child a poor problem solver?

* Does your child have difficulty copying from the board?

Recommendations for working memory problems

* Obtain a positive diagnosis from a doctor, speech pathologist, educational psychologist or other appropriate professional first, and follow their recommendations. These people are invaluable as the key to removing any roadblocks your child may have.

* Get your child off the devices and get them writing by hand. Revisit the chapter dealing with Step 3 for advice on this and why it's important.

* Work on following instructions with them. Start with a single task, then add one more thing, keeping pace with your child's limits until they can handle a number of steps in an instruction.

* Read aloud and recap the events in the stories together, as often as you can. This will help your child with sequencing, retention and comprehension. Revisit the chapters on steps 2, 5 and 6 for more on this.
* Play card games like Memory and Go Fish. Use real cards, not card games on devices. Revisit the chapter on Step 4 as a reminder of why this is important.

Dyslexia

Around 80 per cent of children identified with reading difficulties have dyslexia. It causes problems with reading, spelling and sometimes comprehension. Children with dyslexia have trouble processing speech and recognising words, and they often have problems with their working memories. They struggle with linking the speech sounds in words with their printed versions.

Like all learning difficulties, these problems can range from mild to severe. Professionals consider these two groups most at risk of developing dyslexia: a child from a parent with dyslexia, and a child with a spoken language problem in their early years. If your child falls into one of these groups and you are concerned, seek advice from your doctor or their teacher first. They'll be able to refer you to the right professional for assessment.

Observing your child from preschool and through the primary years and knowing what to look for will help if there is a problem. Observing and collecting information is important if your child eventually needs to be seen by a professional. This checklist shows things you can look out for, but it is not a diagnostic tool, and it's important to remember that children develop at their own rates. Consultation with your child's teacher should be your first step if you're worried.

Signs of possible dyslexia

Preschool

* a slow or late talker with a limited vocabulary for their age
* doesn't recognise their own name in print after repeated teaching
* has trouble writing their name
* often pronounces words in reverse such as 'cream ice' instead of 'ice cream'
* struggles to learn rhymes and nursery rhymes
* has trouble with simple memory tasks, like following a set of directions

Kindergarten–Year 2

* struggles to learn and retain letter names and their corresponding sounds
* slow to learn words and retain a simple word bank of sight words
* confuses simple words like 'to' and 'of'
* confuses letters that look similar, such as *p* and *q*
* has difficulty with tasks that rely on working memory, such as remembering a sequence or verbal explanations and instructions
* poor spelling and trouble recalling spelling rules
* poor reading comprehension
* disinterested and reluctant to do reading and writing activities

Middle to upper primary school

* does not recognise many sight words
* has significant trouble sounding out unfamiliar words
* struggles to complete any literacy tasks

* struggles to explain what happened in a story and has events in the story out of sequence
* does better answering oral questions than ones that they must read
* makes the same mistakes over and over, such as letter reversals or substituting the same incorrect words
* often leaves out words they can't read and tries to skip past them
* reading and writing is at a lower standard than their speaking and thinking skills
* avoids reading and writing

Recommendations for children with dyslexia

* Use the years before school to get children reading-ready. Don't worry about teaching a child to read. If you get them as reading-ready as possible, the rest will follow. You know how to do this because you've read through the seven steps. Most of what's in those chapters can be done as part of your day-to-day activities. Talk and interact with your child to get their speech and language skills up to scratch: read aloud to them, share books with them, sing nursery rhymes with them and get them writing by hand. If you are dyslexic yourself and prefer not to read aloud, revisit page 78 for some alternative approaches.

* Use their preschool years to fine-tune their phonological systems. Work with them in a playful way to recognise rhyming patterns in words, and teach them the sounds for the letters of the alphabet. Have them write the letters of the alphabet, saying the sounds for those letters as they do. Read lots of books with repetition and patterns. Revisit steps 1, 2, 3, 4 and 6 for help with this.

* During their school years, keep the reading aloud going, even if they are struggling to learn to read. This will ensure that their comprehension and vocabulary skills continue to grow while they work on developing their decoding skills. Revisit Step 6 for help with this.

* Minimise the use of technology in the home unless it's for read-aloud experiences and worthwhile sound/letter correspondence work. Children with dyslexia do not need the added problems that too much tech can mean for their brains. Revisit Step 4 for advice on this.

* Once you've spoken with your child's teacher, collected information and tried classroom intervention, seek professional advice and have a full assessment done by a recommended speech pathologist or educational psychologist. Don't let the problems follow your child unaddressed as they progress through school.

Dysgraphia

Dysgraphia is difficulty with written expression. Children with dysgraphia have trouble spelling and putting their thoughts down on paper, and often have poor handwriting. Children with dyslexia often present with dysgraphia as well, but not always; sometimes dysgraphia appears in isolation. There are two types of dysgraphia: language-based and non-language-based.

Children with language-based dysgraphia appear to have trouble getting their ideas down on paper. When they express themselves orally, their thoughts and how they are ordered are always of a much higher standard than what they can manage to get down in written form. So, there is a big disparity between what the mind is capable of and how they can show that on paper.

These children can have problems with sound/letter relationships that affect the way they spell. They might also struggle with correct grammar and punctuation, and will often leave words out. Their actual formation of letters and handwriting is generally legible and of acceptable standards. It is incredibly frustrating for these children, as their ideas are so ordered and advanced, yet getting them from their head onto the paper turns even their most perfectly formed sentences into chaos.

On the other hand, children with non-language-based dysgraphia, sometimes known as motor-based dysgraphia, have difficulty with the actual act of writing. These children struggle to form legible letters, words and sentences, and don't have the fine motor skills needed for writing by hand. They have no trouble constructing sentences and conveying their thoughts on paper in a concise and sequential way, but find the act of writing exhausting and extremely difficult.

This checklist will help you identify if your child might have a form of dysgraphia. It is only a guide for the sort of things to look out for. Follow up by consulting with a professional if your child exhibits several of the points on this checklist.

Does your child:

* have poor spelling?
* confuse their letters regularly?
* have illegible writing?
* have trouble with zips, buttons and scissors?
* hold and grip the pencil in an unusual way?
* position their book, paper or their body in an unusual way when they write?
* have a mismatch between their reading skills and their writing skills?

* have a mismatch between oral and written work?
* have difficulty writing down what they say?
* use poor spacing, an incorrect blend of uppercase and lowercase letters and differing letter sizes within words?
* struggle to hold a pencil and write for even a small amount of time?
* find the process of writing even a simple sentence slow and exhausting?
* avoid writing activities?

Recommendations for children with dysgraphia

Language-based dysgraphia:

* Consult an occupational therapist and follow their advice if your child's writing continues to be illegible by the end of Year 1.
* Encourage your child to record their written expression orally using a recording app.
* Be a scribe for your child.
* Make sure their phonological systems are up to scratch. Work with them to recognise rhyming patterns in words, teach them the sounds for the letters of the alphabet and have them write the letters of the alphabet and say the sounds for those letters as they do. Read lots of books with repetition and patterns. Revisit the seven steps chapters for help with this.
* Seek support in the classroom. It's important that your child continues to write thoughts down on paper and that they receive guidance and help to do this.

Non-language-based or motor-based dysgraphia:

* In the early years, use a multi-sensory approach; that is, more than one sense at a time. Have them write in sand or shape the

letters with Play-Doh, form letters in shaving cream, trace letters and words formed from letters cut from sandpaper for a tactile experience. Revisit chapter four for more on this.

* Make sure tapping, swiping and pinching does not take the place of gripping, scribing and writing in your home.

* Get pencils and pens with proper grip shapes or use pencil grips on all your child's writing implements. Revisit Step 3 for advice on this.

* Consult an occupational therapist and follow their advice if your child's writing continues to be illegible by the end of Year 1.

* As your child moves into high school, if their writing continues to be illegible and is an overwhelmingly exhausting task for them, get them typing and using apps such as SnapType, which will allow them to more easily complete worksheets and activities.

Takeaways from this chapter

* Struggling readers who don't get the intervention they need will not get better at reading, and they will fall further and further behind.

* Early assessment and intervention is the key to academic success and happiness.

* Working memory problems are one of the biggest issues in reading difficulties. When reading, children need their working memories so they can read an unknown word, decode an unknown word, put information they've read into their own words, comprehend what they've just read, problem-solve, retell and sequence events in a story, and follow a set of instructions.

* Around 80 per cent of children identified with reading difficulties have dyslexia.

* Professionals consider two groups most at risk of developing dyslexia: the child of a parent with dyslexia, and a child with a spoken-language problem in their early years.

* Children with dysgraphia have trouble spelling and putting their thoughts down on paper, and often have poor handwriting.

* There are two types of dysgraphia: language-based and non-language-based.

* For any reading difficulties, once you've spoken with your child's teacher, collected information and have tried classroom intervention, seek professional advice and have a full assessment done by a recommended speech pathologist or educational psychologist.

* Don't let any of these reading difficulties follow your child unaddressed into higher year levels.

Notes

That reading thing

1. Anne Kloth, 'Dyslexia: The brain is wired differently', *Reading Success Plus*, 5 July 2016. https://readingsuccessplus.com/dyslexia-the-brain-is-wired-differently/

Step 1: Talking their way to literacy

1. Mitsuhiko Ota, Nicola Davies-Jenkins & Barbora Skarabela, '*Why Choo-Choo Is Better than Train*: The Role of Register-Specific Words in Early Vocabulary Growth', *Cognitive Science*, vol. 42, 2018, pp. 1974–99; Matthew Masapollo, Linda Polka & Lucie Ménard, 'When infants talk, infants listen: pre-babbling infants prefer listening to speech with infant vocal properties', *Developmental Science*, vol. 19(2), 2016, pp. 318–28; Nairán Ramírez-Esparza, Adrián García-Sierra & Patricia K Kuhl, 'Look Who's Talking NOW! Parentese Speech, Social Context, and Language Development across Time', *Frontiers in Psychology*, vol. 8, 2017, p. 1008.

2. Betty Hart & Todd R Risley, 'The Early Catastrophe: The 30 Million Word Gap by Age 3', *American Educator*, vol. 27(1), 2003, pp. 4–9; Jessica F Schwab & Casey Lew-Williams, 'Language Learning, Socioeconomic Status, and Child-Directed Speech', *WIREs Cognitive Science*, vol. 7(4), 2016, pp. 264–75.

3. Make the First Five Count, 'How Does Your Child Speak and Understand Languages?' Easter Seals, Toronto, Canada http://makethefirstfivecount.ca/parent-answers/child-speak-understand-languages/

4. Walter Kintsch & Eileen Kintsch, 'Comprehension', in S G Paris & S A Stahl (eds.), *Children's reading comprehension and assessment* (Routledge: New York), 2005, pp. 71–92.

5. Masooma Sundus, 'The Impact of Using Gadgets on Children', *Journal of Depression and Anxiety*, vol. 7(1), 2018.

Step 2: Reading their way to literacy

1. Maria de Jong & Adriana Bus, 'Quality of book-reading matters for emergent readers: An experiment with the same book in a regular or electronic format', *Journal of Educational Psychology*, vol. 94(1), 2002, pp. 145–155.

2. Ibid.

3. Quoted in Connie Matthiessen, 'The hidden benefits of reading aloud – even for older kids', *GreatKids.org*, 20 July 2013. https://www.greatschools.org/gk/articles/read-aloud-to-children/

4. Penny Sarchet, 'Let them fidget! Squirming around helps children with ADHD focus', *New Scientist*, 11 June 2015. https://www.newscientist.com/article/dn27706-let-them-fidget-squirming-around-helps-children-with-adhd-focus/

Step 3: Linking writing and reading

1. Hanover Research, 'The Importance of Teaching Handwriting in the 21st Century', February 2012.

2. Amelia Hill, 'Children struggle to hold pencils due to too much tech, doctors say', *Guardian*, 26 February 2018. https://www.theguardian.com/society/2018/feb/25/children-struggle-to-hold-pencils-due-to-too-much-tech-doctors-say

3. Karin H James & Laura Engelhardt, 'The effects of handwriting experience on functional brain development in pre-literate children', *Trends in Neuroscience and Education*, vol. 1(1), 2012, pp. 32–42.

4. Marieke Longchamp, Jean-Luc Velay & Marie-Thérèse Zerbato-Poudou, 'The influence of writing practice on letter recognition in preschool children: A comparison between handwriting and typing', *Acta Psychologica*, vol. 119(1), 2005, pp. 67–79.

5. Pam A Mueller & Daniel M Oppenheimer, 'The pen is mightier than the keyboard: Advantages of longhand over laptop note-taking', *Psychological Science*, vol. 25(6), 2014.

6. Dennis Pierce, 'What Is The Relationship Between Reading And Writing? It's Linear', *TeachThought*, January 2018. https://www.teachthought.com/literacy/relationship-between-reading-writing/

Step 4: Taming the tech and making it count

1. Hanover Research, op cit, 2012.
2. Bernard Marr, '5 Important Artificial Intelligence Predictions (For 2019) Everyone Should Read', *Forbes*, December 2018. https://www.forbes.com/sites/bernardmarr/2018/12/03/5-important-artificial-intelligence-predictions-for-2019-everyone-should-read/#7fe891b7319f
3. Manfred Spitzer, *Digital dementia: What we and our children are doing to our minds [Digitale demenz: Wie wir uns und unsere Kinder um den Verstand bringen]* (Droemer Knaur: Munich), 2012.
4. Julian Ryall, 'Surge in "digital dementia"', *Telegraph*, 24 June 2013. https://www.telegraph.co.uk/news/worldnews/asia/southkorea/10138403/Surge-in-digital-dementia.html
5. Adam Gorlick, 'Media multitaskers pay mental price, Stanford study shows', *Stanford News*, August 2009. https://news.stanford.edu/news/2009/august24/multitask-research-study-082409.html
6. Helene Hembrooke & Geri Gay, 'The Laptop and the Lecture: The Effects of Multitasking in Learning Environments', *Journal of Computing in Higher Education*, vol. 15(1), 2003.
7. Joshua S Rubinstein, David E Meyer & Jeffrey E Evans, 'Executive Control of Cognitive Processes in Task Switching', *Journal of Experimental Psychology: Human Perception and Performance*, 27(4), 2001, pp. 763–97.
8. Sundas, 2018, op. cit.
9. Australian Government / eSafety Commissioner, 'eSafety Parents and Carers'. https://www.esafety.gov.au/parents/big-issues/time-online
10. Sarah Vaala & Lori Takeuchi, 'QuickReport: Parent Co-Reading Survey', Joan Ganz Cooney Center at Sesame Workshop, September 2012. Ziming Liu, 'Reading behavior in the digital environment: Changes in reading behavior over the past ten years', *Journal of Documentation*, vol. 61(6), 2005, pp. 700–12.
11. Yuhyun Park Yuhyun, '8 digital skills we must teach our children', *World Economic Forum*, 13 June 2016. https://www.weforum.org/agenda/2016/06/8-digital-skills-we-must-teach-our-children/

Step 5: Harnessing the power of book ownership

1. Mariah Evans, Jonathan Kelley, Joanna Sikora & Donald Treiman, 'Family scholarly culture and educational success: Books and schooling in 27 nations', *Research in Social Stratification and Mobility*, vol. 28(2), 2010, pp. 171–97.
2. Ibid.

3. Ibid.
4. https://nces.ed.gov/surveys/pirls/

Step 6: Embracing two reading philosophies

1. Constance Weaver. *Reading process & practice: From socio-psycholinguistics to whole language* (Heinemann Educational Books: Portsmouth, NJ), 1998, p. 44.
2. Stephen Machin, Sandra McNally & Martina Viarengo, '"Teaching to Teach" Literacy', Centre for Economic Performance discussion paper, April 2016.

Step 7: Finding just-right books for any age

1. Roman Krznaric, 'The Empathy Effect: How Empathy Drives Common Values, Social Justice and Environmental Action', paper written for Friends of the Earth's 'Big Ideas' project, March 2015, p. 3.
2. P Matthijs Bal & Martijn Veltkamp, 'How Does Fiction Reading Influence Empathy? An Experimental Investigation on the Role of Emotional Transportation', *PLoS One*, vol 8(1), 2013; Raymond A Mar, Keith Oatley & Jordan B Peterson, 'Exploring the link between reading fiction and empathy: Ruling out individual differences and examining outcomes', *Communications*, vol. 34(4), 2009, pp. 407–28.
3. https://www.ncacl.org.au/ncacl-cultural-diversity-database/
4. Barack Obama & Marilynne Robinson, 'President Obama & Marilynne Robinson: A Conversation—II', New York Review of Books, 19 November 2015. https://www.nybooks.com/articles/2015/11/19/president-obama-marilynne-robinson-conversation-2/
5. Scholastic Australia, *Kids and Family Reading Report*, 2016, p. 56. http://www.scholastic.com.au/readingreport/home.html
6. American Academy of Pediatrics, 'Giving books to kids before summer break can stem reading losses', *Science Daily*, 25 April 2015. www.sciencedaily.com/releases/2015/04/150425215624.htm.

About the author

Louise Park began her career as a primary-school classroom teacher, and then moved into teaching literacy to primary-school students for whom English was a second language. She holds a Masters degree in children's literature and literacy, and has worked as a literacy advisor to disadvantaged schools, a presenter of guided reading and writing seminars, and an education publisher. She has written numerous teaching modules and has scoped, created and collaborated on some of the biggest English and literacy programs sold worldwide today, including *Bookshelf* and *Reading Discovery*.

These days, Louise spends her time writing books for children – sometimes under the pseudonyms H I Larry, Mac Park and Poppy Rose – and presenting in schools as well as at festivals and conferences. She is the ambassador for the Bright Futures Are Written by Hand campaign, a Books in Homes role model, and a Littlescribe author.

Louise loves nothing more than battling beasts, catching naughty dinosaurs on the loose, testing out gadgets as a boy spy, time travelling and hatching new ideas for books that just might grab a reader and hook them in the way she was hooked as a child. For she knows that a child that gets hooked on reading will grow into a reader, and that a reader has more doors open to them in this world.

www.louisepark.com.au